ENTERPRISE AND ENTREPR

1.1 ENTERPRISE AND ENTREPRENEURSHIP

Section 1.1 focuses on the dynamic nature of business and why and how new business ideas come about. The impact of risk and reward is examined alongside the role of business enterprise.

1.1.1 THE DYNAMIC NATURE OF BUSINESS

What you need to know

Why new business ideas come about (changes in technology, changes in what consumers want, products and services becoming obsolete)

How new business ideas come about (original ideas, adapting existing products / services / ideas)

Businesses operate in dynamic market places, as the products that customers want and need change constantly. The businesses that can adapt to the changes which are happening around them, are the ones that are most likely to be successful.

Each decision a business makes uses resources, in terms of time and/or money. It is, therefore, important that every decision is carefully considered to take account of any changes that are expected to happen in the future or to deal with any change that is happening now. This will help to ensure that businesses can survive and continue to evolve and grow. Those businesses that stand still and do not change with the times will find it increasingly difficult to sell products that are in demand. This may ultimately result in business failure.

Why new business ideas come about

There are different reasons why new business ideas come about.

Changes in technology

Technology is constantly changing. This creates opportunities for businesses to take risks and develop new products which make use of the most modern technology. This may prove successful, as in today's society many consumers demand products that utilise the most up-to-date technology, as these products may offer more convenience in everyday life. Those businesses that ignore advances in technology and stand still are more likely to be unsuccessful in the long-term, as their products may become out-of-date or obsolete.

Changes in what consumers want

Over time, consumer needs and wants change. Businesses that can adapt their product offerings or set up new business enterprises to capitalise on these changes are more likely to be successful.

Products and services becoming obsolete

Some products and services become out of date as consumers no longer demand them. Technology may have moved on or it may be that consumers can buy a similar or superior product elsewhere more conveniently. Online banking, for example, has resulted in many high street bank branches closing. Businesses that constantly look at developing new products and services that match customer needs more exactly than existing product offerings are likely to thrive and grow. Those businesses that continue to sell out-of-date products, despite falling demand, will struggle to generate sales long-term and may eventually fail if they do not adapt.

How new business ideas come about

An entrepreneur is an individual who sets up and runs a new business and, therefore, take on the risks associated with that business.

Entrepreneurs can generate business ideas by spotting possible gaps in the market. This means that they may see an opportunity to develop a good or service that is not already produced by another business. Other business ideas are formed by entrepreneurs believing they can offer a superior product to what is already available to buy on the market.

Original ideas

A key characteristic of many entrepreneurs is creativity. Entrepreneurs will often produce many original ideas for new goods and services. In many cases, these will not prove practical or profitable to develop on a larger scale and take to market. Some ideas, however, will be worth pursuing, researching and developing further. It is very difficult to come up with original and new ideas for products and services and it is estimated that 8 out of 10 new products fail. However, if an entrepreneur or business can develop a new idea successfully, and on an ongoing basis, it can gain a competitive advantage.

Adapting existing products / services / ideas

Many new products are developed from existing goods or services, whereby the entrepreneur thinks of a way of making improvements. This process makes it quicker and cheaper compared to launching brand new products. This is because less research and development is required and a business may already have the equipment to make a product that is similar to an existing one. There is, therefore, much less risk involved in adapting a product that already exists compared to investing in an original idea. Adapting existing products can also help a business protect its main or core products by bringing out revised versions. This can keep consumer interest and sales high.

 Exam Gold You must ensure that you understand why and how business ideas come about. If a question on this topic area is linked to a specific case study in the exam, you must make sure you relate the business theory you have covered to the specific circumstances featured in the case. This is vital to gain the marks for application, as there are very few marks available for just demonstrating knowledge in certain parts of the exam papers. Despite demonstrating correct knowledge, answers that are generic or not linked to the case will score no marks for AO2 or application.

1.1.2 RISK AND REWARD

What you need to know

The impact of risk on business activity (business failure, financial loss, lack of security)

The impact of reward on business activity (business success, profit, independence)

Setting up a new business is risky, as things do not always go to plan. Risk is all about chance. Through planning, the risk of making a particular decision can be reduced. Planning and, as a result, reducing risk can involve carrying out and using reliable market research, monitoring costs carefully and reviewing business performance to ensure that the business is progressing and meeting its set targets within an appropriate timescale. Through successfully taking risks, entrepreneurs may then gain rewards.

The impact of risk on business activity

There are several different types of risk that an entrepreneur can face when setting up a business.

Business failure

The largest risk for any entrepreneur is that the business will ultimately fail, meaning that it no longer trades or exists. This is a very significant risk, as over half of all business start-ups fail within the first five years, resulting in the time, effort and money invested in the business being lost. This may have an impact on personal relationships, as setting up and running a business means many personal sacrifices, such as working long hours and, therefore, less time spent with family and friends.

Financial loss

Depending on the type of business the entrepreneur decides to set up, the entrepreneur may be responsible or liable for all the debts of the business if it fails. As a result, the entrepreneur may need to sell personal possessions, such as jewellery, a car or even a house, in order to find the money to pay off these debts.

If an entrepreneur sets up a business as a limited company, the owners or shareholders of the business will only lose the money they have invested in the business if it fails. This limits the amount of financial loss to the entrepreneur and business owners.

Lack of security

When setting up a business, an entrepreneur may be giving up a regular wage or salary as an employee for another business. Employees will have a sense of security that bills can be paid when needed. This feeling of security can be lost when setting up a business, as the predicted sales and costs that a business is expected to generate may differ in reality. This may result in the entrepreneur having concerns about whether the business will be able to trade into the future and whether the entrepreneur will be able to take a decent wage from the business and have the standard of living that is desired.

The impact of reward on business activity

An entrepreneur can experience many rewards for setting up a business. It is the drive to succeed and experience these rewards that results in entrepreneurs taking and overcoming the risks in setting up a business, to find ways to provide goods and services that are in demand.

Business success

Business success can be measured in many different ways. The fact that a business has survived past its first year or is making enough profit for the business owner(s) to have a decent standard of living may be seen as a success by the entrepreneur(s). The value of sales and/or profit and the share of the market the business holds in terms of sales are all different ways of measuring business success.

An entrepreneur may have set personal objectives of opening and running a successful business. Building an enterprise from scratch, making the first sale, employing more people and helping the local community are all factors that can give an entrepreneur a personal sense of satisfaction and excitement when running a business and would, therefore, be seen as other examples of success.

Profit

If the amount of money that a business makes from selling its products, otherwise known as revenue, is higher than the costs of running the business, the entrepreneur will make a profit. When setting up a business, the profits that are generated are usually low or even non-existent. However, as a business grows there is an opportunity to make larger profits, which may be higher than any wages or salary gained from being employed at another business. If the business is very successful, then large returns can be generated.

Independence

Being in full control of a business and having the ability to make all the decisions is a reward for many entrepreneurs when running a business. This level of independence can be very self-satisfying, particularly if the entrepreneur is headstrong and does not like taking orders or instructions from others.

Exam Gold Do not assume that every business that opens up will succeed. Remember, some businesses will fail. In an exam, look at the case study carefully to determine the specific risks and rewards that an entrepreneur has experienced when setting up. Remember, risk is all about chance and careful planning can reduce the risk involved in setting up a business. If a business is not doing well, can you determine from the case study why this may be happening?

A successful entrepreneur will weigh up the chances and implications of success and failure before setting up a business.

1.1.3 THE ROLE OF BUSINESS ENTERPRISE

What you need to know

The role of business enterprise and the purpose of business activity (to produce goods or services, to meet customer needs and to add value: convenience, branding, quality, design, unique selling points)

The role of an entrepreneur (organise resources, makes business decisions, takes risks)

The role of business enterprise and the purpose of business activity

The term 'enterprise' has two common meanings. Firstly, an enterprise is simply another name for a business. Secondly, the word enterprise describes the actions of someone who takes a risk by setting up, investing in and running a business.

Someone who shows enterprise by setting up a business is called an entrepreneur.

To produce goods and services

Products can be broken down into goods and services. Goods are physical or tangible products that people can touch, such as a table, television or sofa. Some goods last a long time, whereas others do not, such as fresh fruit and vegetables.

Services are intangible and non-physical items, such as hairdressing, nursing or a train journey.

In order to be successful, entrepreneurs must produce goods and services that are in demand or, in other words, people must want to buy them. If there is no demand for the products, then the business will not generate any sales and therefore will not be successful. The entrepreneur must also be able to produce goods and services cost efficiently, to ensure that the business can make a profit through the money generated from selling the goods being higher than the costs to produce them.

To meet customer needs

To be successful, a business should identify customer needs and then aim to meet these needs better than rival businesses.

Customer needs and wants differ. Customer needs are more essential and make people's lives more comfortable when they are provided. Products that aim to meet customer wants compete with other products for customers to spend their spare money on. Small, independent businesses can meet customer needs and wants successfully if they offer a more convenient service compared to larger businesses.

To add value

In order to make a profit, an enterprise will need to sell its products at a price that is higher than the costs of making the product. This is known as 'added value.' Added value is the difference between the cost of inputs required to make the product, such as raw materials, and the price that customers are willing to pay for it. Value can be added to a product by increasing the price or reducing the costs. Businesses aim to add value to the products they produce. This will allow them to pay for their other costs from the value added, such as rent, lighting and insurance and then go on to, hopefully, make a profit.

There are 5 main ways of adding value:

1 Convenience

People are more inclined to pay more for a product if it makes their lives easier and saves time.

2 Branding

A brand is a unique design, symbol, sign or word(s) that can be used separately or together in order to create an image of a product or business. A strong, positive brand can differentiate the product/business from rivals. This can add value and people may be prepared to pay more for a product that is associated with that brand.

3 Quality

Quality is about meeting customer expectations. Customers will have an expectation of the quality of a product and the more a product meets or exceeds this expectation, the more value will be added in its production and, therefore, the higher the price that can be charged.

4 Design

How easy a product is to use, as well as its physical appearance can both add value to a product. Additional value can be added to a product if costs are kept to a minimum when designing.

5 Unique selling points

If a product is different to its rivals in a way that is seen as positive by its customers, such as an adding an additional feature, then the business may be able to charge a higher price, as people will be prepared to pay more for it.

The role of entrepreneurship

Entrepreneurship is the pattern of behaviour of entrepreneurs, for example, being innovative, organised, determined and resilient. An entrepreneur has many roles when setting up and running a business.

Organise resources

The entrepreneur will organise the resources required to produce the goods and services they intend to sell. This includes recruiting any staff to help the entrepreneur when running the business, choosing suitable premises to operate the business from and buying or renting equipment needed to operate the business successfully.

Make business decisions

The entrepreneur must make well thought through decisions that are ideally based on information rather than gut feeling or instinct. This lowers the risk of the wrong decision being made. However, time is of the essence when setting up and establishing a business and, therefore, too much pondering about which course of action to take may result in an opportunity being lost to rivals.

Take risks

An entrepreneur is a calculated risk taker. Every decision an entrepreneur takes involves risk. The business world is dynamic and changeable and, therefore, there is a degree of uncertainty when decisions are made. Not every decision will be the right one, but in taking risks and showing resilience to move on when not everything goes the entrepreneur's way, gives the entrepreneur the opportunity to gain rewards.

 Exam Gold Every business was initially set up by an entrepreneur and you should recognise the role and qualities of the entrepreneur from any business case study that you read in the Paper 1 exam.

Added value is a key business concept and is likely to be regularly assessed. Make sure you understand the different ways of adding value in that some are physical, whereas others are in the mind of the customer, such as branding. Remember: the higher the value added, the greater the chance the business has of making a profit.

SPOTTING A BUSINESS OPPORTUNITY

1.2 SPOTTING A BUSINESS OPPORTUNITY

Section 1.2 focuses on the importance of identifying and understanding customer needs. The purpose, methods and the use of data in market research is examined together with how businesses use market segmentation to target customers. The competitive environment is also considered.

1.2.1 CUSTOMER NEEDS

What you need to know

Identifying and understanding what customer needs are (price, quality, choice, convenience)

The importance of identifying and understanding customers (generating sales, business survival)

Identifying and understanding what customer needs are

In order to be successful, a business will need to identify and understand customer needs. This will then allow an entrepreneur to produce the goods and services that customers want and demand, which will then help the business to survive and grow in the future. Customer needs are constantly changing and businesses need to be aware of these changes and respond appropriately with their product offerings.

Customer needs can be broken down into four categories.

Price
Customers will expect to pay a reasonable or acceptable price for the products they wish to buy. The actual price charged can vary based on the quality, timing, delivery arrangements and the popularity of a particular product.

Quality
Customers will want the products they buy to meet or exceed their own expectations and requirements of quality. This may not necessarily be the highest quality, as customers may be happy with a cheaper product of a reasonable quality. There is a link between the level of quality of a product and the price charged. If a product is seen by customers to be of a high quality in relation to rival products, a higher price can be charged by the business, as customers may feel this level of quality is worth the price.

Customers tend to aim to obtain the highest level of quality for a price that is seen as acceptable when buying products.

Choice
Most customers would like a choice or a range of options when buying products. If choice exists, it is more likely that their needs as customers will be met more exactly with the product they choose to buy. Choice can exist in terms of different brands, different quality and price combinations and different varieties of the same product. If lots of choice exists, it usually results in high competition in the market, which can equal lower prices.

Convenience
In today's society, customers increasingly want products that make their lives easier. Products that save people time are increasingly popular, as modern lifestyles are busy, juggling work, leisure and other commitments. People are more inclined to pay more for a product if it makes their lives easier and saves time.

The importance of identifying and understanding customers

Generating sales

A business that successfully identifies customer needs and produces a good or service that meets those needs successfully, better than rivals, will experience higher demand. They will, therefore, be able to sell large volumes of their products, which will mean high sales revenue for the business.

Business survival

A business will have more chance of survival in a competitive market through generating larger sales than rivals through meeting customer needs more exactly.

 Exam Gold Identifying and understanding customer needs is a fundamental part of business. You must recognise the importance of a business continuing to adapt its products to changing customer needs. A business that does not do this may eventually fail, as customers will no longer have so much interest in its products. Look carefully at the case studies given in the exam to determine whether a business is thriving or experiencing difficulties because it is or is not meeting customer needs successfully.

1.2.2 MARKET RESEARCH

What you need to know

The purpose of market research (to identify and understand customer needs, to identify gaps in the market, to reduce risk, to inform business decisions)

Methods of primary market research (survey, questionnaire, focus group, observation)

Methods of secondary market research (internet, market reports, government reports)

The use of data in market research (qualitative and quantitative data, the role of social media in collecting market research data, the importance of the reliability of market research data)

The purpose of market research

The aim of market research is to gather information. Collecting market research data should be an ongoing process to inform business decision-making.

To identify and understand customer needs

Customer needs can be identified and understood through collecting market research. With this information, goods and services that a business then produces should match customer needs more exactly. For smaller businesses, feedback from customers may be gained through regular face-to-face contact. However, with larger businesses, this feedback may not be so readily available and, therefore, market research will be vital to ensure products match what customers actually want.

To identify gaps in the market

Market research can identify if customer needs are being met by existing products or whether gaps exist that could be filled through the development of new products. If a gap is identified, and market research shows that it may be worthwhile to produce a new good or service to fill that gap, then businesses should move quickly to take advantage of this opportunity before rivals.

To reduce risk

Basing business decisions on market research helps to reduce risk and costly mistakes, as there is more certainty of the outcomes of these decisions.

To inform business decisions

Market research provides information to businesses to ensure that decisions made by managers are based on data rather than gut feeling. This increases the chances that the decision will be well thought through and will be the right one.

Methods of market research

Primary research

Primary research involves obtaining data first hand to match the specific needs of the business.

Advantages	Disadvantages
• Up-to-date and first hand • Matches the needs of the business exactly	• Time consuming and expensive • Large sample size required for results to be representative and valid

Survey

Surveys are a way for businesses to find information out about their target market. This may be through a form of questionnaire, possibly online. These usually contain closed questions i.e. questions where different options are given to the respondents (the people answering the survey) to choose from.

Advantages	Disadvantages
• Large amounts of data can be collected and analysed relatively easily • Online surveys are easy to conduct on a regular basis	• The sample (the group of people that take part in the survey) must reflect the profile of the target market for the results to be valid

Questionnaire

There are different types of questionnaire that businesses can use.

Type of questionnaire	Advantage	Disadvantage
Postal – sending questionnaires directly to the homes of people the business wishes to find views from	• Can be sent anywhere the business chooses • Can distribute to a large sample	• Low response rate, as often seen as junk mail • An incentive may need to be given to encourage the questionnaire to be returned
Face-to-face – asking questions directly to respondents	• Body language and mood can be noted • Unclear questions can be clarified or visual aids shown	• Low response rate, as people do not wish to be disturbed • Time consuming to gain a representative sample
Telephone – contacting respondents directly through the phone to complete a series of set questions	• Cheap compared to a postal questionnaire • Can be administered on a large scale	• Low response rate, as people do not wish to be disturbed in their own home • Time consuming to gain a representative sample

Focus group

A focus group is where a small number of actual or potential customers are brought together to discuss a product or a market.

Advantages	Disadvantages
• In depth, qualitative data can be collected • Gives an insight into customer perceptions and behaviour	• Small sample size, therefore, the views may not be representative of a larger sample • Time consuming to conduct • Subject to bias of the interviewer

Observation

Footfall, customer behaviour or rival businesses can be observed.

Advantages	Disadvantages
• Observe behaviour directly, rather than asking respondents to recall events • Less bias as observations take place in a natural setting	• Time consuming • Needs to be conducted at different times and on an ongoing basis to ensure that valid results are gained

Secondary research

Secondary research involves using data that already exists and has been produced for a different purpose.

Advantages	Disadvantages
• Quick to administer as information is readily available • Generally cheaper than primary research and at times can be free	• Can be out of date • May not fit the exact needs of the business

Internet

A wealth of information can be found on the internet, for example, reviewing rival websites, looking at cost information or market trends.

Advantages	Disadvantages
• Large amounts of information is readily available • Cheap	• Information overload • Information may be inaccurate or out of date

Market reports

Organisations such as Mintel and Keynote produce a wide variety of reports that analyse individual markets in depth, such as future trends in market size or the main players in a market.

Advantages	Disadvantages
• Large amounts of information is readily available • A general overview of a market can be gained	• Expensive • Information is general rather than specific about local markets

Government reports

The Government produces a wealth of information that is accessible on the internet.

Advantages	Disadvantages
• Information is provided from a trusted source • Free	• Can be lengthy and, therefore, time consuming to read • May be difficult to extract and understand information that is relevant

The use of data in market reserach

Qualitative and quantitative data

Qualitative data	This information is specific and cannot easily be converted into numerical data. It is based on opinions, feelings and attitudes from a small number of people through focus groups or interviews.
Quantitative data	Numerical data that can be analysed statistically. It is usually based on large sample sizes through the use of questionnaires/surveys. It, therefore, may be more reliable for a business to use than qualitative data.

Effective market research will enable a business to make more informed decisions, therefore creating less risk. Businesses will usually link the quantitative and qualitative findings of their research together to help create a picture of likely customer preferences and behaviour, enabling the business to identify, anticipate and meet customer needs and wants more effectively. This will increase the chances of business success.

The role of social media in collecting market research data

Social media is becoming increasingly important when collecting market research data. Feedback from Facebook and Twitter accounts allows a business to find out views about itself and/or its products extremely quickly. In addition, social media allows a business to respond instantly to customer feedback and use private messaging functions to find out more information if necessary.

Advantages	Disadvantages
• Users are actively engaged with the comments process • Positive interactions with customers can lead to higher levels of brand loyalty	• Negative comments can be viewed by many and can, in extreme cases, go viral • Experience and time is required to manage social media accounts effectively

Potential customers may look at TripAdvisor reviews before visiting a hotel, attraction or restaurant. These reviews provide a way of customers providing honest feedback that others can read about their experiences. These reviews can then influence the decision of potential customers as to whether to use the business or not. It is, therefore, important that a business tries to provide the best experiences for its customers at all times, to ensure the reviews are positive and more sales can be gained.

The importance of the reliability of market research data

Important business decisions will be made on the basis of market research and, therefore, it is vitally important that it is reliable. Reliability will mean that the results provide a more realistic picture, for example, the research reflects the views of the whole target market accurately.

However, a balance needs to be maintained between the cost and time and the accuracy of the research that is collected. It is very unlikely that a small business will be able to afford, or the entrepreneur will have the skills to carry out, detailed market research. A compromise will, therefore, need to be taken by the business.

The following factors should be considered to ensure that any market research conducted is as reliable as possible:

Bias	A small sample size may mean the results gathered through market research do not accurately represent the views of others in the market. Larger sample sizes are more difficult to conduct and are expensive, but the results should contain less bias.
Up to date	Data collected should be as current as possible to ensure that business decisions are made on the most accurate and valid information.
Accuracy	Questions and instructions need to be clear to avoid misinterpretation.

 Exam Gold Market research is a commonly examined topic area. You must ensure that you are clear on the different research methods that are available to businesses and ensure that, if you are asked to choose an appropriate research method in the exam, that it is suitable for the type and size of the business that is referred to.

It is also important to keep up-to-date with how technology increasingly influences the ability of businesses to collect and respond to information.

It is worth remembering that there are always problems with conducting market research and careful consideration should be made of the limitations and problems of using different methods.

1.2.3 MARKET SEGMENTATION

What you need to know

How businesses use market segmentation to target customers (identifying market segments: location, demographics, lifestyle, income, age, market mapping to identify a gap in the market and the competition)

How businesses use market segmentation to target customers

To identify market segments

Market segmentation is the process of dividing a market into groups or segments of people based on different and distinct characteristics. Businesses will then target their products at a specific group of customers rather than aiming to target the whole market.

The groups of people found within a market segment will have shared needs and wants and, therefore, should respond in a similar way to any marketing activity. This will allow the business to allocate time and resources specifically to this group, increasing efficiency. As a result, promotional activity is more likely to be personalised to the specific market segment, leading to higher sales and a greater chance of success.

Market segmentation will take place after market research.

There are five main ways in which a market can be broken down into segments.

Location

This is where the market is divided up by area. This could be as wide as a country or continent, for example the "European market." Small businesses, however, may just focus on a local area to target their products. The people in a particular area may have common characteristics and, therefore, would be interested in specific goods and services. For example, independent designer shops may choose to locate in an area which has many expensive houses and high income earners.

Demographics

Demographics is a study of the population based on factors such as age, gender, marital status, family size, race, nationality and religion. Some of these factors are covered separately in this section. Demographics is one of the most common ways of segmenting a market, as each group will have specific characteristics and their own patterns of spending.

Lifestyle

Potential consumers are grouped into segments based on factors such as their interests, hobbies, marital status, religious views and political opinions.

Income

Income levels determine how much customers can spend on goods and services. Businesses can segment a market by reviewing the annual or monthly income levels of particular groups. By a business then choosing to target high income, mid-income or low income earners, it can then produce goods and services at a price that have a better chance of being in demand.

Age

Not all products are used by all, or equally by all, age groups. Segmenting a market by age group is an effective way that businesses can personalise its products and create better and more targeted promotional campaigns.

Market mapping to identify a gap in the market and the competition

Market mapping is a way of identifying if any gaps exist in a market where customer needs are not currently being met by existing products.

A market map comprises two axes which represent key features of the market, for example, high to low price, high to low quality, younger to older customers. The existing products in the market are then plotted to identify if any gaps exist. If a gap is seen to exist in the market map, the business must be careful to ensure sufficient demand will exist for a product that fills the gap. Some gaps will not be worth pursuing, such as a low-quality product that is charged at a high price. This can be determined through market research.

 Exam Gold Market segmentation is a key topic area in business. A business that does not segment its market and tries to aim its products at everyone is very likely to fail. Small businesses have a greater chance of success against larger rivals if they understand the distinct characteristics of the market segment they are targeting.

It is very important that you understand the different methods of market segmentation that exist and the benefits of market mapping, as these topic areas are commonly assessed in Edexcel papers.

1.2.4 THE COMPETITIVE ENVIRONMENT

What you need to know

Understanding the competitive environment (strengths and weaknesses of competitors based on: price, quality, location, product range and customer service, the impact of competition on business decision making)

Understanding the competitive environment

Competition exists when two or more businesses are selling products independently of each other to the same target group of customers. Businesses will try to produce a good or service where they do not face much, if any, competition. However, in reality, all businesses will have some form of competition. This competition might be strong and direct, i.e. there are many businesses producing very similar products, or indirect i.e. competitors are producing goods or services that represent an alternative way for consumers to spend their money.

The competitive environment refers to the strength of competition between businesses in the same market.

Strengths and weaknesses of competitors

A business can compare itself to the relative strengths and weaknesses of its rivals in many different areas. Through conducting an analysis of its rivals, a business can assess the impact of competition and, as a result, make better and more informed decisions.

Price

A business can compare its prices to its rivals and how much value the price represents in terms of the product being sold.

Quality

Customers expect the quality of a product to meet or exceed their expectations. A business that does not provide a product of the right quality will find it very difficult to attract and retain customers.

Location

The location of a business can have a massive impact on the number of customers and sales it generates compared to rivals. A small business that is located in an area with a higher passing trade than a rival, which is located in a more out of the way location, is likely to attract more customers and generate more revenue. However, premium locations are often very costly and a new, small business must look at its finances carefully to determine whether it can afford to pay the high rents on an ongoing basis.

Product range

The number of products one business has compared to its rivals is important to consider. A business must ensure that it is meeting the needs of its target market fully with its product range. If a rival is doing this better, a business will lose out on sales and market share.

Customer service

Customer service can enable a business to differentiate itself from rivals. High levels of customer service can result in higher levels of customer satisfaction. This can increase brand loyalty and reduce the impact of competition on sales.

The impact of competition on business decision making

The presence of competition forces a business to be the most efficient it can be, so that costs can be kept to a minimum and prices can then be kept low. Competition also encourages innovation and progress. Businesses operate in dynamic markets and those that stand still and do not constantly review the needs of their customers, by offering quality products in comparison to rivals, will find it difficult to survive in the long term.

Businesses will need to monitor competition carefully, as it will affect many important decisions business owners will need to make.

Exam Gold Nearly all businesses face competition. Rival firms will have a large impact on the decisions that firms make.

In the exam, when assessing a business featured in the case study, it is important to review the strengths and weaknesses of competition in comparison to the business to determine why one business is performing better than another. Referring to the actions of competitors in an appropriate and relevant way will almost always help you gain context marks, a common area of weakness in student responses.

PUTTING A BUSINESS IDEA INTO PRACTICE

1.3 PUTTING A BUSINESS IDEA INTO PRACTICE

Section 1.3 reviews some of the practical aspects of running a small business. It focuses on what business aims and objectives actually are and specifically the business aims and objectives of a start-up business. The reasons why aims and objectives differ between businesses are also examined. The concept and calculation of revenue, costs, profit, interest and break even are covered alongside the interpretation of break even diagrams. The importance of cash and the calculation and interpretation of cash-flow forecasts are explored, together with the different sources of finance that are available to use in a start-up or an established small business.

1.3.1 BUSINESS AIMS AND OBJECTIVES

What you need to know

What business aims and objectives are

Business aims and objectives when setting up (financial aims and objectives: survival, profit, sales, market share, financial security; non-financial aims and objectives: social objectives, personal satisfaction, challenge, independence and control)

Why aims and objectives differ between businesses

What business aims and objectives are

An aim is a broad target that a business will set out to achieve. Objectives set out how a business plans to achieve its aims. In order to be effective, objectives need to be SMART i.e. Specific, Measurable, Achievable, Realistic and Time-bound. This means that managers can easily see if objectives have or are being met and, if not, appropriate action can then be taken. For this reason, careful monitoring of aims and objectives must be undertaken on an ongoing basis to measure how successful the business is at meeting them.

Aims and objectives provide a clear direction for businesses and as a result they give a sense of purpose to employees, which increases motivation. Decisions taken within the business should all, therefore, help in one way or another to meet its aims and objectives.

Business aims and objectives when starting up

Financial aims and objectives

Financial aims and objectives specifically relate to the money in the business. Financial aims and objectives are interlinked.

Survival

Survival is the main focus when a business is starting up. A new business may have produced a business plan detailing the expected costs and revenue, but in reality, customer numbers may be lower and costs higher than expected. This may be down to a new competitor unexpectedly opening, a supplier increasing its prices or the entrepreneur basing decisions on unreliable market research. This will severely impact the cash coming into and out of the business. If a business is unable to pay its day-to-day bills, as it does not have enough cash readily available to use, the survival of the business may be threatened.

Profit

In the short-term, it is unlikely that a start-up business will be able to make a profit, due to the high costs of setting up or revenue being lower than expected. However, in the long-term, making profit will be the main objective for most businesses. This is the reward to the entrepreneur for their hard work and the risks undertaken. Ideally, the profit earned is sufficient to provide the entrepreneur with enough income to live on. Profits may also be kept in the business by the owner for expansion or further development.

Sales

Some new businesses will set targets linked to sales rather than profit when first setting up. Concentrating on sales will help the name of the new business become more widespread, leading to an increased volume of sales and sales revenue. Focusing on sales may help a business to build up relationships with its customers. This may increase brand loyalty, repeat business and sales in the future.

Market share

New businesses will aim to get a foothold in the local market where they are opening in order to gain market share.

Market share is the percentage of the total sales a business currently generates. The higher the market share, the more power the business has in its market in terms of setting prices. There is also a greater chance that other firms will want to stock the products of the business.

Sales and market share objectives are closely linked. Establishing and building market share may be more of a priority for a new business start-up rather than trying to be profitable. Focusing on market share will help to ensure the business is able to make profit in the future.

Financial security

Having financial security that a business will pay more than a securely paid job, or that it will significantly increase the entrepreneur's wealth in the longer term, is an objective of many business start-ups. To achieve financial security, new businesses should look to increase their market share, which will increase their power in the market, as well as protect their ideas from being copied by others. By establishing a unique product, a business is much more likely to survive, generate sales, increase market share and in the long term generate profit, as it will be suitably different from rival businesses.

Non-financial aims and objectives

Non-financial aims and objectives are not linked to money. For some entrepreneurs non-financial aims and objectives are more important than financial aims and objectives.

Social objectives

Setting up businesses that help others, otherwise known as not-for-profit organisations, are increasingly important in today's society. When setting social objectives, the entrepreneur is thinking about more than just profit. Decisions and objectives will be set to help meet the needs of key stakeholder groups (individuals who are interested or are affected by a business). Charities are good examples of organisations that set social objectives, as they have a clear cause in society that they wish to improve.

Personal satisfaction

Many entrepreneurs aim to gain a feeling of personal satisfaction when setting up a business. It is the achievement of building something from scratch and working independently, rather than for an organisation as an employee, which may motivate the business owner.

Challenge

Setting up a new business poses many challenges to an entrepreneur and they must show strong character and resilience to persevere if not every aspect of setting up and running the business goes to plan. Some people thrive on this type of challenge and will experience high levels of satisfaction if the business succeeds.

Independence

Many entrepreneurs want the freedom and independence to make their own decisions rather than being told what to do by others. They may have felt when working as an employee that their skills were not recognised or used fully. Setting up a business will therefore give the business owner more of an opportunity to fulfil their own potential.

Control

Control is linked to independence. Setting up a business means that the entrepreneur has all the power to make the decisions and therefore is in full control of the business. This is a huge motivator, as the entrepreneur will have the freedom to run the business in whichever way they deem best.

Having full control over the business also enables the entrepreneur to have the flexibility to work when it is convenient and to choose holidays when it suits. However, remember many entrepreneurs find it difficult to switch off and take a break from work, as setting up a business is extremely time consuming and challenging.

Why aims and objectives differ between businesses

Every business and entrepreneur is different and this is the main reason why aims and objectives differ between businesses. Some entrepreneurs will only be motivated by sales and profits, whereas others may be more concerned with helping others. In this case, they will set targets to meet this goal. The external environment and the level of competition a business faces will also have an impact on the specific aims and objectives that different businesses set.

In today's dynamic business world, those firms that focus not just on financial aims and objectives but on non-financial ones as well, are likely to be more successful now and in the longer term. Many consumers today are interested in the impact a firm has on society and the environment when producing and selling its products. Those businesses that fail to consider non-financial aims and objectives are likely to fall behind rivals operating in the same market.

Exam Gold It is extremely important that you recognise which aims and objectives are classed as financial and which are categorised as non-financial. This topic area lends itself easily to a multiple choice or short answer question and many students would be caught out thinking that survival is classed as a non-financial objective. Revise this section carefully so that you do not fall into this common trap!

It is also important that you remember not every business just wants to make a profit. There are many different aims and objectives that a business can set; profit is just one of them and, again, this is a common misconception of many students.

1.3.2 BUSINESS REVENUES, COSTS AND PROFITS

What you need to know

The concept and calculation of: (revenue, fixed and variable costs, total costs, profit and loss, interest, break even level of output and margin of safety)

Interpretation of break even diagrams (the impact of changes in revenues and costs, break even level of output, margin of safety and profit and loss)

The concept and calculation of:

Revenue

Formula: REVENUE = PRICE X QUANTITY

Revenue is the value of the money the business makes from selling its products.

Worked Example 1

Business X has provided some financial information shown in the table.

Sales price per unit	£40
Number of units sold	100

To calculate total revenue:

1 Multiply the sales price per unit by the number of units the business has actually sold.
For Business X this is £40 x 100 = **£4,000**

Exam Gold It is important to remember that revenue is not profit. Many students get these two concepts muddled. As you will see later in this section, the costs of a business must be deducted from the revenue before profit can be calculated.

Fixed costs

Fixed costs do not change as output varies. Even if a business makes more units or products, the fixed costs of the business will stay the same. There are many examples of fixed costs including rent, salaries, insurance and interest repayments. A fixed cost will not stay the same forever, it can change over time. For example, the rent a business pays may be reviewed and increased after a set period.

Variable costs

Formula: TOTAL VARIABLE COSTS = VARIABLE COST PER UNIT X OUTPUT

Variable costs directly change when output changes. The higher the output, the higher the variable costs. Common examples include raw materials, bought in stock or component parts, packaging and wages based on hours worked or the amount produced.

Total costs

Formula: TOTAL COSTS = TOTAL FIXED COSTS + TOTAL VARIABLE COSTS

Total costs are calculated by adding together the total fixed costs to the total variable costs of the business.

Worked Example 2

Business X has provided some additional financial information.

Variable cost per unit	£15
Salaries	£1,000
Rent	£400
Number of units sold	100

To calculate total costs:

1 Identify which costs are fixed and which are variable.

2 Add the fixed costs together, as these do not change with output. In this case, the fixed costs are salaries and rent. Fixed costs, therefore, amount to £1,000 + £400 = **£1,400**

3 Multiply the variable cost per unit to the number of units sold, as total variable costs will increase as more output is produced.
For Business X, the total variable costs would equal £15 x 100 = **£1,500**

4 Add the total fixed costs and the total variable costs together to find the total costs.
Business X total costs = £1,400 + £1,500 = **£2,900**

Exam Gold Price and cost are two key terms that are often used by students interchangeably and, as a result, sometimes incorrectly. It is worth remembering that the price is the amount customers are willing to pay for a product. Cost is the amount spent by the business to make the product that it is selling. The cost of producing a product has a direct impact on the price of the product and the amount of profit that can be earned from each sale.

Try not to fall into this trap and double check your work to ensure that you are using the correct term in the correct context every time.

Profit and loss

Formula: PROFIT = TOTAL REVENUE – TOTAL COSTS

Having calculated its total costs and total revenue, a business can now work out its profit. Profit is the difference between costs and revenue. If costs are greater than revenue then a business will make a loss. However, if the revenue of a business is greater than the costs, then it will make a profit.

Profit is the financial return the owners of a business aim to achieve to reward themselves for the risk they have taken in starting up a new enterprise. However, the owners may choose not to take all of the profit out of the business for their own gain. Some profits may be kept in the business for reinvestment and growth.

Many new businesses find it difficult to make a profit when they first set up. This may be because the business has not become well known in the area and sales are growing slowly. It may also be because costs are higher than expected and/or the start-up costs of the business may have been very high.

Worked Example 3

To calculate the profit for Business X:

1 Calculate the revenue of the business, in this case £4,000

2 Calculate the total costs of the business, which were £2,900 for Business X

3 Deduct the total costs from the revenue i.e. £4,000 - £2,900 = **£1,100**

4 **£1,100** represents the profit Business X has made during the time period the figures relate to

Interest

Formula: INTEREST ON LOANS (%) = $\dfrac{(\text{TOTAL REPAYMENT} - \text{BORROWED AMOUNT}) \times 100}{\text{BORROWED AMOUNT}}$

Interest is the cost of borrowing and/or the reward for saving and is expressed as a percentage.

When setting up a business, an entrepreneur may need to borrow money in the form of a loan or a mortgage. A mortgage is a type of loan that is organised with the bank in order to buy a property or building. The entrepreneur may also arrange an overdraft facility with the bank. An overdraft enables the business to access additional cash when needed to pay its day-to-day bills. These sources of finance will require interest to be paid when, and if, they are used. Interest charges will be included in the total costs of the business.

Worked Example 4

A new business start-up borrowed £50,000 from a bank. Over the lifetime of the loan, the business repaid £60,000 in total. Calculate the percentage interest on the loan.

To calculate the percentage interest on the loan:

1 Substitute the figures from the question into the formula above.

2 The total amount the business repaid to the bank including interest equalled **£60,000**.

3 The amount the business initially borrowed was **£50,000**.

4 Subtract the value of the total repayment from the borrowed amount.
   In this case, £60,000 - £50,000 = **£10,000**

5 Divide this amount by the initial amount borrowed i.e. the £50,000 and multiply by 100 in order to calculate a percentage
   $\dfrac{£10,000}{£50,000} \times 100 = \textbf{20\%}$

The interest on this loan as a percentage is 20%. This means that the business will repay the value of the loan, £50,000, plus an extra 20% of this amount as interest.

Worked Example 5

A business intends to borrow £12,000 from the bank. The business will repay the loan over four years and its monthly repayment will be £275.90. Calculate the total interest the business will pay for this bank loan as a percentage of the total amount borrowed. Give your answer to two decimal places. You are advised to show your workings.

To tackle this question:

1 Write down the loan amount which in this case is **£12,000**.

2 Work out the number of months the business will make repayments on the loan:

12 months x 4 years = **48 months**

3 Calculate the value of the repayments the business will make over the lifetime of the loan:

£275.90 x 48 months = **£13,243.20**

4 Calculate the value of the interest the business will pay in total, by deducting the loan amount from the total value of the repayments:

£13,243.20 − £12,000 = **£1,243.20**

5 Substitute the figures into the formula to work out the total interest as a percentage of the total amount borrowed:

$$\frac{£1,243.20 \times 100}{£12,000} = \textbf{10.36\%}$$

Concept and calculation of break even level of output and interpretation of break even diagrams

Break even level of output

Formula: BREAK EVEN = TOTAL COSTS = TOTAL REVENUE

Break even is where total revenue is equal to total costs. At this point, the business is not making a profit or a loss. Through calculating break even, a business knows how many units it will need to produce and sell in order to start making a profit.

This information can be represented on a break even diagram and will show the potential profit or loss that could be made at different levels of output, as revenue and costs change.

In order to construct a break even diagram, a business will need to know the value of its:

1 Fixed costs

2 Variable cost per unit

3 Sales price per unit

A break even diagram or graph shows the total revenue and total costs of a business at different possible levels of output. A break even diagram for Business Z is shown below:

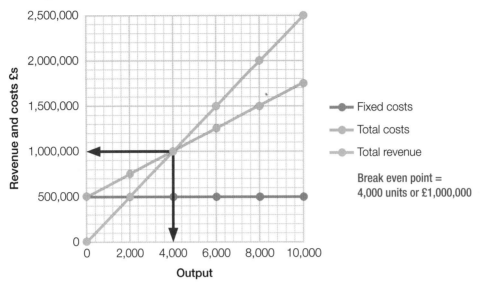

There are three lines plotted on the break even diagram shown: fixed costs, total costs and total revenue at different level of sales or output. Costs and revenues are plotted on the y axis in pounds and the number of sales/output is plotted on the x axis.

Worked Example 6

Steps to draw a break even diagram:

1 Calculate the value of the total fixed costs of the business. Remember, regardless of how many units will be made or sold, the value of fixed costs will remain the same. The value of fixed costs for this business is £500,000.

2 Calculate the value of total variable costs, by multiplying the variable cost per unit at different levels of output. The variable cost per unit for Business Z is £125.00 and the volume of output ranges from 0 to 10,000 units.

Output	Variable cost per unit	Total variable costs
0	£125.00	£0
2,000	£125.00	£250,000
4,000	£125.00	£500,000
6,000	£125.00	£750,000
8,000	£125.00	£1,000,000
10,000	£125.00	£1,250,000

3 Calculate the total costs of Business Z, by adding the total fixed costs to the total variable costs at the different levels of output.

Output	Total variable costs	Total fixed costs	Total costs
0	£0	£500,000	£500,000
2,000	£250,000	£500,000	£750,000
4,000	£500,000	£500,000	£1,000,000
6,000	£750,000	£500,000	£1,250,000
8,000	£1,000,000	£500,000	£1,500,000
10,000	£1,250,000	£500,000	£1,750,000

4 Calculate the value of total revenue at different levels of output. The sales price that Business Z intends to charge its customers per unit is £250.00.

Output	Sales price per unit	Total revenue
0	£250.00	£0
2,000	£250.00	£500,000
4,000	£250.00	£1,000,000
6,000	£250.00	£1,500,000
8,000	£250.00	£2,000,000
10,000	£250.00	£2,500,000

5 Decide on your scale for the x and y axes. Look at the highest value that you will need to plot. In this case, it is revenue at £2,500,000. This is highest value you will need on your y axis. The highest possible level of output for the business is 10,000 units. This is, therefore, the point where the x axis needs to end. It is important to make your scales easy to read and use when drawing break even diagrams.

6 Plot the total revenue line. This will start at zero and will increase diagonally. This is because as the business makes and sells more, it will gain more revenue.

7 Plot the fixed cost line. Fixed costs are drawn as a straight, horizontal line as they do not change with output.

8 Plot the total cost line on the graph. The total cost line is plotted instead of the variable cost line on its own, as the total cost line considers both fixed and variable costs. The total cost line starts at the same point as fixed costs, as even if the business is making no output, fixed costs still need to be paid. At zero output, however, variable costs are zero, resulting in fixed costs and total costs being the same value.

9 The point where total revenue and total costs intersect is the break even point. In this example, the break even point of the business is 4,000 units or £1,000,000. These figures can easily be seen from the graph itself. This means that if the business manages to produce and sell this amount of output, it will not make a profit, but, equally, it will not be in a loss making situation. It will be breaking even.

Profit and loss

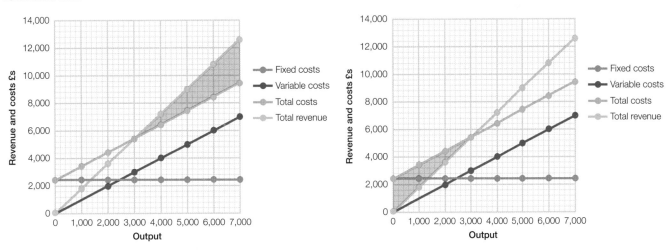

A business can calculate the amount of predicted profit or loss it expects to make at different levels of output from the break even diagram. Profit is calculated by deducting total costs from total revenue.

The two shaded areas on the break even diagrams above represent the areas of profit and loss for the same business. The break even point is 3,000 units. The triangle or wedge that is shaded in the first diagram is the area of profit. At 3,001 units and above the business will be making some sort of profit, as it has passed its break even point and the total revenue line is higher than the total cost line.

In the second diagram, the area before the business has reached its break even point is shaded. Looking at the diagram, it can be seen that the total cost line is higher than the total revenue line at output levels 0-2,999 units. As the business has not yet reached its break even point, it will be making a loss.

Worked Example 7

Business Z wishes to know what the predicted profit or loss will be if it operates at 8,000 units.

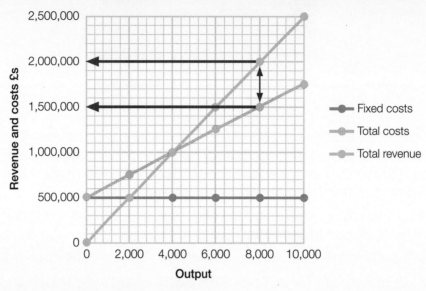

To calculate the profit or loss at 8,000 units for Business Z:

1. Identify from the break even diagram the value of total revenue at 8,000 units. To do this, look along the x axis until 8,000 units is found, find the appropriate point on the revenue line and read the value across on the y axis. In this case, the value of revenue is **£2,000,000**.

2. Follow the same process as step 1, but this time read the value of the total costs figure at 8,000 units which is **£1,500,000**.

3. Deduct the total costs figure from the total revenue figure to work out the predicted profit at that level of output. For Business Z, this would be £2,000,000 - £1,500,000 = **£500,000**.

4. **£500,000** is the predicted profit that the business will make at this level of output.

This process can be repeated for any level of output shown on the break even diagram. However, the difficulty is that sometimes values are tricky to read from the diagram. Therefore, if a business relied solely on this method for calculating profit, inaccurate figures may be used, which would impact on decision making. For example, looking again at the break even chart for this business, it is difficult to accurately work out the profit or loss at an output level of 9,000 units only using the diagram.

Exam Gold Remember, when calculating profit and loss from a break even diagram, if the break even point has not yet been reached the business must be making a loss. This can easily be seen as the total cost line will be higher than the total revenue line.

Negative figures in business are always written in brackets rather than with a minus sign.

Margin of safety

Formula: MARGIN OF SAFETY = ACTUAL OR BUDGETED SALES – BREAK EVEN SALES

The margin of safety is the difference between the current level of output/sales of a business and its break even point.

Worked Example 8

If Business Z was operating at 10,000 units and the break even point is 4,000 units, the margin of safety is calculated as:

10,000 units (current level of output) – 4,000 units (break even point) = **6,000 units**

The management at Business Z would want the margin of safety to be as high as possible, as this shows how much output or sales could fall before the business hits its break even point. There is less risk to a business when the margin of safety is high that it will end up in a loss-making situation.

Exam Gold The margin of safety can be calculated by using the break even diagram and also the formula. By using the diagram, managers will be able to see visually how comfortable a position the business will be in when operating at different levels of output.

The impact of changes in break even diagrams

As well as calculating profit and loss and identifying the break even point, the break even diagram can also be used to help business owners with decision making and "what if" scenarios. By changing one or more variables in the break even diagram, business owners, or business decision-makers, can then assess the impact of any change(s) on the break even point. This will allow worst and best case situations to be prepared for.

Worked Example 9

Business Z wishes to see the effect on the break even point if the sales price per unit was lowered from £250.00 to £200.00 per unit.

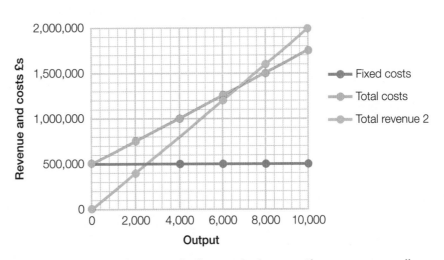

For this question, the break even diagram can be either redrawn, as in the graph above, or the new revenue line can just be replotted on the existing graph. Business managers can then read from the break even diagram, the new break even point in units and in value and compare this to the original break even point.

In this example, the break even point is 6,667 units. This means by lowering the sales price per unit, the break even point will rise by 2,667 units. As a result, Business Z will have to sell more units before it will break even and go on to make a profit. However, the lower price may result in more demand, so this break even point may be reached quicker compared to the lower break even point at the higher sales price.

Exam Gold This example shows one of the limitations of break even diagrams in that is difficult to read, with 100% accuracy, the new break even level of output at 6,667 units.

Always be careful when reading break even diagrams that you look at the axes carefully to ensure you are reading the figures as accurately as possible. The figures may not be represented so clearly as £500,000 or £1,000,000. Figures may be represented as 500 with (£'000s) shown on the y axis.

Break even level of output

Formulae: BREAK EVEN IN UNITS = $\dfrac{\text{FIXED COSTS}}{\text{(SALES PRICE – VARIABLE COST)}}$

BREAK EVEN POINT IN COSTS/REVENUE = BREAK EVEN POINT IN UNITS X SALES PRICE

Rather than drawing a break even diagram to calculate the break even point each time, a quicker and more efficient method of calculating break even is to use the formula.

In order to calculate break even in units using the formula, three variables are required.

These are fixed costs, sales price and variable cost per unit.

Worked Example 10

To calculate break even in units for Business Z, the total fixed costs are predicted to be £500,000. The original sales price per unit, before the price change, is £250.00. The variable cost per unit is £125.00.

Substituting this into the formula:

$$\frac{£500,000}{(£250.00 - £125.00)} = \frac{£500,000}{£125.00}$$

= 4,000 units

This answer matches the value of 4,000 units from the break even diagram.

Worked Example 11

To calculate the value of break even in costs/revenue, the break even point in units is required, as well as the sales price per unit.

Substituting the figures for Business Z into the formula given:

4,000 units x £250.00

= £1,000,000

This again corresponds with the same value at the break even point on the "y" axis for costs/revenue in £s on the break even diagram.

Exam Gold If a question asks you to calculate break even, make sure you read the question carefully to see whether it asks for break even in units or costs/revenue. Learn all the formulae carefully, as none will be given in the exam.

Calculating break even using the formulae is much quicker than drawing a break even diagram. Remember, you will not be required to draw a break even diagram in the exam. You will need to show that you can identify the break even level of output and margin of safety from a break even diagram. You will also need to interpret the impact of changes in revenue and costs on break even diagrams.

We have covered break even diagrams in depth here to ensure you have a full understanding of the concept, as it is a topic area many students find difficult.

Exam Gold Every calculation question in the exam will be worth two marks and will advise you to show your workings when you are completing your answer. This is important, so that the examiner can see your method when they are assessing your work. It is also important as, by writing down the workings, you are much more likely to calculate the answer correctly, so it will help you to avoid making errors in your calculations.

It is absolutely vital that you write your final answer on the line that is given in the answer template. Examiners are trained to look at this line first to see if the correct answer is there. If it is not, the examiner will then look at the workings provided. One mark will only be awarded for a mathematical slip or for not fully following the demands of the question, for example, an answer is given to one decimal place rather than two.

It is also advised not to put more than one answer in the answer box. Even if the correct answer is there, but it is not clear that this is your final answer (as it is not written on the answer line and/or it is surrounded by other figures or other answers) you will not be awarded any marks at all.

1.3.3 CASH AND CASH-FLOW

What you need to know

The importance of cash to a business (to pay suppliers, overheads and employees, to prevent business failure (insolvency), the difference between cash and profit)

Calculation and interpretation of cash-flow forecasts (cash inflows, cash outflows, net cash flow, opening and closing balances)

The importance of cash to a business

Cash refers to the money available in a business to spend.

To pay suppliers, overheads and employees

Without sufficient cash, the business may struggle to pay day-to-day bills and this may threaten the survival of the business.

The main payments a business must make are to:

- Suppliers, to pay for stock. This may involve immediate payment when the stock is first received by the business. Alternatively, the supplier may offer the business trade credit. This helps the cash position of the business, as the firm will have an opportunity to sell the stock before it has to pay for it. Many new businesses, however, find it difficult to arrange trade credit with their suppliers as the suppliers are wary that many new firms fail, which, if this happens, may result in no payment.

- Overheads, expenses that are not directly related to making a product. Overheads must be paid on an ongoing basis for the business to keep trading. Examples include the payment of rent, insurance and utility bills, such as gas and telephone.

- Employees, who must be paid their wages or salaries on time. Employees who worry they may not be paid at all or, if they are regularly paid late, may decide to leave the business to find a job with more financial security.

To prevent business failure (insolvency)

Insolvency is a situation where a business cannot pay its bills on time. Having sufficient cash and not having too much debt will help a business avoid insolvency. If a business cannot regularly pay its bills on time or it cannot negotiate an extension for repayment with its creditors (businesses that it owes money to), then it is very likely to fail. A business cannot operate without staff, stock, lighting, heating etc.

The difference between cash and profit

Cash is not the same as profit. Cash refers to the amount of money that a business has available to spend at a particular moment in time. Many profitable businesses fail because they do not have enough cash to pay their bills. This is because profit is recorded straight after a sale, whereas cash is recorded when it is either spent or received by a business. If a business offers trade credit to a customer, for example, 30 days, then the sale and, therefore, profit are documented when the goods are taken by the customer. However, the cash will not be recorded by the business until payment is received i.e. when the cash is received 30 days later.

Calculation and interpretation of cash-flow forecasts

Cash-flow is the movement of money into and out of a business. A cash-flow forecast predicts this movement of money over a future time period and will show its likely effect on the bank balance of the business. Cash-flow forecasting is important for every business, particularly those that experience seasonal patterns of demand, such as ice-cream shops, those firms that are growing quickly and new business start-ups.

Making accurate predictions of the flow of money into and out of the business is extremely difficult for business managers to do. This is especially the case for new businesses which may have limited experience of operating in their markets. Poor cash-flow is a major reason why many new businesses fail.

Cash inflows

Cash inflows refer to the movement of money coming into the business. These are also called receipts and include items such as the receipt of a bank loan and revenue generated from cash sales and credit sales.

Cash outflows

Cash outflows refer to the movement of money going out of the business. These are also called payments and include all items that the business must pay for such as rent, salaries, stock, advertising and loan repayments/interest.

Net cash flow

Formula: NET CASH FLOW = CASH INFLOWS – CASH OUTFLOWS IN A GIVEN PERIOD

Net cash flow is the difference between the cash inflows and cash outflows.

Worked Example 1

A business has predicted the following financial information for January.

	January (£)
Total cash inflows	6,000
Total cash outflows	4,000
Net cash flow	**2,000**

In this example, the business is predicted to have a net cash flow of £2,000 in January. This figure is calculated by deducting the forecast total cash outflows away from the forecast total cash inflows. As this figure is positive, it is called a surplus and is a strong position for the business to be in.

Worked Example 2

Another business has predicted the following financial information for January.

	January (£)
Total cash inflows	3,000
Total cash outflows	8,000
Net cash flow	**(5,000)**

This example shows a different situation. In January, the business is forecasting £3,000 in total cash inflows. However, it is anticipating that total cash outflows will equal £8,000. As these outflows are expected to be larger than the total inflows, the net cash flow is forecast to be £5,000 deficit. If the predictions are correct, a negative cash-flow shows that the business will not have enough cash in the business to cover its payments. If the business has organised an overdraft or other funds to cover this period of deficit, then the business will be able to continue to trade. However, if the business has not foreseen this difficulty and is unprepared, it may not be able to raise any more cash. In this case, the business will struggle to continue to operate, as it will be unable to pay its day-to-day bills.

 Exam Gold It is important to remember that the terms "profit" and "loss" should not be used when referring to cash-flow. A positive and negative closing balance in the cash-flow forecast should be referred to as a surplus or deficit, respectively. Profit and cash are two different concepts.

Opening and closing balances

Formula: OPENING BALANCE = CLOSING BALANCE OF THE PREVIOUS PERIOD

The opening balance is the amount a business expects to have in its bank account on the first day of the period the figures relate to. The opening balance will always be the same figure as the closing balance of the previous period.

Formula: CLOSING BALANCE = OPENING BALANCE + NET CASH FLOW

The closing balance is the amount a business expects to have in its bank account on the last day of the period and is calculated by adding the values of the opening balance and the net cash flow together for the same period.

 Exam Gold You may be asked to calculate figures from a cash-flow forecast in the exam. Remember to always show your workings and write your final answer on the line provided in the answer template where the appropriate units will be already be given, for example, £s, %s.

Worked Example 3

A business has provided a cash-flow forecast for the first six months of next year.

£'000	January	February	March	April	May	June
Cash inflows	200	250	200	150	100	250
Cash outflows	250	300	300	100	250	150
Net cash flow	(50)	(50)	(100)	50	(150)	100
Opening balance	250	200	150	50	100	(50)
Closing balance	200	150	50	100	(50)	50

This cash-flow forecast shows that the closing balance always becomes the opening balance for the next period or month, as indicated by the shaded boxes in January and February. The opening balance is added to the net cash flow for the period, which may be a positive (April) or negative (May), in order to calculate the closing balance for that month. The closing balance each period might be a surplus, a positive cash balance at the end of the month, or a deficit, a negative cash balance at the end of the month. This is indicated by brackets, as in May.

This cash-flow forecast shows that the business will start the six-month period in January with a cash surplus, or opening balance, of £250,000. During the first three months, the net cash flow is negative, as it is predicted that there will be more cash outflows than inflows, which will reduce the closing balance surplus to £50,000 in March. In April and June, the cash outflows are estimated to reduce considerably making them less than the cash inflows, resulting in a surplus in the closing balance in those two months. In May, again, the outflows are predicted to be higher than the cash inflows. The opening balance, of £100,000, is not enough to cover this increase and therefore the business is forecasted to go into a deficit of £50,000 in that month. Business managers will need to look at the cash-flow forecast carefully and see where potential issues lie for the business.

It is important that businesses predict when they are likely to go into deficit so that they can make plans to overcome and improve their cash-flow position.

In this case and for many businesses, this may be through:

- Organising an overdraft to cover any shortfalls in cash. For this business, it may be wise to negotiate a bank overdraft of more than £50,000 (if it were possible) to cover any inaccuracies in predictions of the inflows and outflows
- Reviewing the cash outflows to determine whether they can be reduced
- Re-organising any trade credit periods so that cash comes into the business from customers before it leaves the business to pay suppliers

 Exam Gold Remember, the production of a cash-flow forecast is not a guarantee of good cash-flow. Managers should keep comparing actual figures to predicted figures on a cash-flow forecast to ensure that an accurate picture of the cash position of the business is always known. If there are significant differences between the actual and the forecast figures, business managers can then take appropriate action to help overcome any issues.

1.3.4 SOURCES OF BUSINESS FINANCE

What you need to know

Sources of finance for start-up or established small business (short-term sources: overdraft and trade credit, long-term sources: personal savings, venture capital, share capital, loans, retained profit and crowd funding)

Sources of finance for a start-up or established small business

Sources of finance refers to the different ways money can be raised by a business. Businesses need finance to start-up, to keep the business going on a day-to-day basis and for growth and development. The most appropriate source of finance that a business should use depends upon:

- What the money is needed for
- How much is required
- How quickly and for how long the finance is needed
- How expensive the source of finance is
- Whether the business owner is prepared to give up some control over the running of the business

Sources of finance can be split into short-term and long-term.

Short-term sources

Short-term sources of finance fund the day-to-day running of the business and are usually repayable within a year.

Overdraft

An overdraft is an agreement with the bank for a business to withdraw funds from its account that exceed the available cash balance, up to an agreed maximum limit. In this situation, the bank account of the business would become overdrawn, otherwise known as "going into the red." The money provided from the overdraft does not flow into the bank account but is available cash for the business to use if it needs additional funds on a temporary, short-term basis.

Advantages	Disadvantages
• Flexibility, a business can use the overdraft only when it needs additional funds • Interest is only paid when the overdraft facility is used	• Expensive to use on an ongoing basis due to the high variable interest rates charged • The bank can withdraw the overdraft facility at any time

Trade credit

A supplier provides goods to a business but is willing to wait for payment until a later date, possibly up to three months.

Advantages	Disadvantages
• Helps improve cash-flow, as the business has the opportunity to make revenue from selling its products before it must make payment	• Difficult for new start-up businesses to organise, as suppliers usually want to limit their risk and, therefore, request payments up front • The business can gain a bad reputation if it does not make payments on time, which may result in losing future credit arrangements with supplier(s)

Exam Gold Sources of finance is a topic area that is commonly assessed in the exams. You must ensure that you select appropriate sources of finance that relate to the specific needs of the business. Overdrafts and trade credit are not suitable sources of finance to fund large projects or expansion plans. Short-term sources of finance are very much used to tide the business over to keep it running on a day-to-day basis.

Long-term sources

Long-term sources of finance tend to be spent on large projects that a business will pay back over a number of years.

Personal savings

An entrepreneur invests money from his/her own bank account into the start-up business. By using this source of finance, entrepreneurs provide a strong signal to other potential investors and the bank of the commitment they have to their business.

Advantages	Disadvantages
• Does not need to repaid • The entrepreneur keeps full control over the business	• Amount available may be limited • If the business fails, the amount invested may be lost which can put a strain on the entrepreneur's personal situation

Venture capital

This source of finance can relate to either share and/or loan capital. High risk new business start-ups frequently use venture capital if alternative sources of finance are not available. Venture capitalists are often interested in this type of business, as there may be an opportunity to gain a high return if the business idea all goes to plan.

Advantages	Disadvantages
• Access to large amounts of funds which may not be available elsewhere • Potential access to expert advice from the venture capitalist	• Possible loss of ownership and control over the business • Loans may need repaying at higher rates of interest than banks would charge

Share capital

Small or new businesses can decide to set up as a private limited company. This type of business can raise finance by selling shares to friends and family members. Each share sold represents a unit of ownership of the business. For example, one person or shareholder decides to buy ten shares in a business which has a total of 100 shares, whereas another person or shareholder buys 20 shares. The shareholder who owns 20 shares, owns 20% of the business and will receive double the amount of dividends (share of the profits, if the business decides to issue a dividend in that accounting period) compared to the other shareholder, who owns 10% of the business. Each shareholder will also have voting rights or power over decision-making in proportion to the number of shares that they own.

Advantages	Disadvantages
• Funds are permanently invested in the business • No interest or repayments need to be made	• Loss of control over the business as the number of shareholders increases • Increased dividend payments resulting in less money available for reinvestment

Loans

A loan is an amount of money borrowed for a set period of time with an agreed repayment schedule. Loans are usually organised with a bank. The repayment amount will depend upon the size and duration of the loan and the rate of interest charged. Loans can be in the form of mortgages, which are large loans issued by banks to help pay for properties. Other loans may be repaid over a number of years, usually between three to ten years, and will be for varying amounts. Small and new businesses often find it difficult to organise a loan with the bank, as the bank will want reassurance that the money can be successfully repaid. Business owners would, therefore, need to draw up a business plan before approaching a bank to request a loan.

Advantages	Disadvantages
• Financial planning may be easier, as repayments are made in regular instalments • No control is lost over the business	• Repayments include interest, therefore, the business will pay more back than it originally borrowed • Security that loan repayments will be made may need to be given to the bank on some of the assets of the business

Retained profit

Instead of the business owners taking the profit out of the business for their own personal gain, they can decide to keep the profit within the business for reinvestment. This is called retained profit and is used by the business for growth and development.

Advantages	Disadvantages
• No interest or repayments • Does not dilute the ownership of the business	• The amount available may be low and therefore business growth can be slow • Retaining too many profits can anger shareholders who will receive a lower dividend payment as a result

Crowd funding

Crowd funding allows small businesses or projects to raise money from a wide range of outside investors online through publicising their idea or proposal. The investors will generally sympathise with the aims of the project or the cause which will encourage them to invest.

Advantages	Disadvantages
• Acts as a way to gauge the popularity of the idea through monitoring the amount of investment that is generated • Low cost investment	• Investors often need an incentive to invest such as a part share in the business, a share of the profits or a free gift • It is difficult for many businesses to gain the required amount

Exam Gold It is vital that you learn the differences between short-term and long-term sources of finance. This area of the specification lends itself very well to multiple choice, short answer and extended response questions. This means that you must carefully select the appropriate source of finance that meets the demands of the question set. For example, share capital would not be a suitable source of finance for a sole trader to use, unless it was thinking of changing its business ownership to a private limited company.

You must also ensure that if you are asked to "explain," "analyse" or "discuss" the pros and cons of a particular source of finance, the points that you give are very specific to the individual source in the question. Vague points that could relate to a number of different sources may not be awarded many, if any, marks.

MAKING THE BUSINESS EFFECTIVE

1.4 MAKING THE BUSINESS EFFECTIVE

Section 1.4 focuses on some of the key decisions that small businesses will need to make when starting up, including the type of ownership and the location of the business. The importance of the four elements of the marketing mix is explored together with how each element must work together. The main components of business plans are investigated, alongside the purpose of planning business activity.

1.4.1 THE OPTIONS FOR START-UP AND SMALL BUSINESSES

What you need to know

The concept of limited liability (limited and unlimited liability, the implications for the business owner(s) of limited and unlimited liability)

The types of business ownership for start-ups (sole trader, partnership, private limited company, the advantages and disadvantages of each type of business ownership)

The option of starting up and running a franchise operation (the advantages and disadvantages of franchising)

The concept of limited liability

When an entrepreneur sets up a business, they will need to think carefully about the type of business ownership or legal structure that the business should take. A key consideration in this decision is the concept of limited and unlimited liability. Liability means who is legally responsible for something.

Limited liability and the implications of limited liability for the business owners

Limited liability is a situation whereby if a business fails, the owners of the business will only lose the money that they have invested already to pay off any debts. The owners will not have to sell their own personal assets, such as their cars or houses, in order to clear these debts. In this way, there is less personal risk of setting up a business which has limited liability.

Unlimited liability and the implications of unlimited liability for the business owners

With unlimited liability, there is no distinction between the owners of the business and the business itself, legally and for tax purposes. This can result in a lack of continuity; if the business has just one owner and they die, retire or decide to sell the business, the business automatically ceases to trade.

The lack of separation between the owners of the business and the business itself also means that the owners are legally responsible for all the debts of the business. This is a huge risk, as many business start-ups fail and any debts that remain will need to be paid off, possibly with the owners' personal funds if there is not enough money in the business to clear them.

 Exam Gold Limited and unlimited liability are two business terms that are commonly confused. Ensure that you use these terms carefully when writing your answers.

The types of business ownership for start-ups

Entrepreneurs have three different choices of business ownership when setting up a new business. Limited and unlimited liability will be a key consideration in their final choice.

Sole trader

A sole trader is a business that is set up and run by one person. This type of business has unlimited liability. Common examples are hairdressers, window cleaners and independent coffee shop owners.

Advantages	Disadvantages
• Owner has full control over decision-making • Very easy and quick to set up	• Unlimited liability • Increased stress, as full responsibility for running the business falls upon one person

Partnership

A partnership is formed where two or more people join together to set up a business to pursue a common purpose. Common examples are vets, doctors and solicitors. In most partnerships, a Deed of Partnership is drawn up which sets out the rules of the partnership, such as how the profit will be split and how decisions will be made, in a legal document. This type of business ownership usually has unlimited liability.

Advantages	Disadvantages
• More owners to contribute funds to the business • Increased knowledge and specialisms	• Unlimited liability • Slow decision-making, as partners are consulted

Private limited company

A company is formed when a business is set up to have a separate legal identity from its owners, which means that the finances of the company are separate from the personal finances of the owners. The owners in this type of business are known as shareholders, who each own shares in the business. As a reward for being a shareholder, the owners will receive a share of the profits, known as a dividend which are paid in proportion to the number of shares that they own. If the company goes bankrupt, shareholders are protected by limited liability.

Private limited companies are run on a day-to-day basis by a Board of Directors, appointed by the shareholders. In small businesses, the shareholders will likely also act as the directors and will make all the decisions on a daily basis. Private limited companies must have at least one shareholder. Additional funds can be raised from the sale of shares to other investors, such as friends and family, but not from the general public. These funds are permanently invested in the business.

Advantages	Disadvantages
• Limited liability • Control can be maintained over the business through the restrictions on who can buy shares	• Increased paperwork and costs of start-up and auditing of accounts each year • Business accounts are not kept 100% private

Exam Gold There are two types of limited company that exist, public limited and private limited companies. Public limited companies will be covered in Theme 2 and, therefore, it is important to remember that private limited companies are only assessed in Theme 1. In most cases, private limited companies tend to be much smaller than public limited companies. Many new business start-ups choose to set up as private limited companies because there is less financial risk for the business owners.

It is also important to remember that a business can only become a company after it has become incorporated, which results in the business gaining limited liability and a separate legal identity to the owners. Students often use the terms 'company' and 'business' interchangeably. A sole trader or partnership should not be referred to as a company, but a business, firm or enterprise.

The option of starting up and running a franchise operation

Franchising is where a business, otherwise known as a franchisor, allows another person or business to trade under its name. This person or business is called a franchisee. Franchising means that entrepreneurs do not have to come up with original business ideas themselves. They use the business format of the franchise including its products, marketing and are allocated a specific location by the franchisor to operate from.

The franchisee pays a fee to the franchisor for the right to trade under its name. The franchisee will also pay the franchisor a percentage of its revenue each year, which are called royalties.

The advantages and disadvantages of franchising

Franchisor

Advantages	Disadvantages
• Expansion without the risk; the franchisee will be funding the growth of the business • Control over major decisions is retained	• Reputation can be affected by a poor choice of franchisee • Not all profits are gained

Franchisee

Advantages	Disadvantages
• Higher chance of business success through a tried and tested business model • Advice, support and training is available from the franchisor	• Ongoing payment of royalties limits amount of profit available • Do not have full control over all business decisions; many major decisions are made by the franchisor

Exam Gold Theme 1 is based on new business start-ups and small businesses. It is important that you revise franchising in light of setting up a new business. Franchising is one of the best ways for an entrepreneur to start their own business, as there is a significant reduction in risk operating under an established brand name. Once the entrepreneur has developed the skills in running their own franchise, they can then go on to set up their own independent business at a later date if they wish to, where they would have the complete freedom to make their own decisions and keep all the profits from themselves.

However, it is worth remembering that not every franchise is a success. Entrepreneurs should research franchise opportunities carefully before investing in one.

1.4.2 BUSINESS LOCATION

What you need to know

Factors influencing business location (proximity to market, labour, materials, and competitors, nature of the business activity, the impact of the internet on location decisions: e-commerce and/of fixed premises)

Factors affecting business location

Once an entrepreneur has found a potentially profitable business idea, a suitable business location will need to be found.

There are many factors that an entrepreneur will need to consider when deciding on the final location of the business and cost will be a huge influence on the decision. Most business start-ups have limited financial resources and, therefore, will want to minimise their set-up costs. Rent is a running cost that will need to be paid on a continual basis; keeping rental costs down will give the business a better opportunity to compete on price. Having a physical location will mean the business will also have to pay business rates. If the entrepreneur decides to buy the premises, it is highly likely that they will need to make repayments with interest on a mortgage.

The other main location factors that an entrepreneur may need to consider when choosing a location are explored below.

Proximity to market

Some businesses may need to be located near to their customers, particularly those that provide services. This allows the target market to easily access the business, which may increase demand, sales volume and, therefore, revenue.

Proximity to labour

Access to a reliable supply of suitably skilled staff is important for some businesses to operate successfully. If it is difficult to recruit or employ the right type of staff in the right numbers, the business will struggle to operate and function efficiently.

Proximity to materials

A business may depend on supplies of a particular raw material to produce its goods, so costs will be lower if the business is located near the supplier. For example, where the raw material is grown or where a distributor is based. This is particularly the case for manufacturing businesses where raw materials may be larger than the finished products themselves. In this situation, it will be much cheaper for a business to transport smaller products than the larger raw materials required to produce the product.

Proximity to competitors

Whether it is best to locate or not locate close to rival businesses depends upon the type of business itself. If there are no competitors in the local area, it may be because the location is not a profitable location for that type of business to operate in. Careful consideration will need to be taken as to why no competitors may exist in a particular area and if there will be sufficient demand to make the business start-up viable.

For other businesses, it will be important to locate near competitors so that customers can have choice. Clothing and shoe stores located in shopping centres or restaurants clustered together are good examples of businesses that prefer to locate near to each other.

 Exam Gold Proximity means how close something is.

Remember, to revise carefully all terms listed in the specification. Any key term or phrase listed in the specification can be included in an exam question. If you are unsure of the meaning of a key term, ensure you endeavour to find it out and then learn the definition.

Nature of the business activity

The specific location factors that are the most important for a particular business will largely depend upon the nature of the activity of that business. Manufacturing businesses will need to locate near to their raw materials, suitably skilled staff and have strong road links to ensure easy transportation of their final products. Alternatively, businesses that provide services will need to locate close to their customers to ensure their services can be provided efficiently.

The impact of the internet on location decisions

The increasing popularity of the internet has resulted in more and more businesses setting up and operating purely online to capitalise on the high growth of sales made through e-commerce and m-commerce. For a business, this can make the physical location less important that the products it sells.

E-commerce and/or fixed premises

If a business operates purely online, then it will not need to pay expensive rents for a central location in a city centre if direct and frequent access to customers is not required. Dependent on the nature of the business, the entrepreneur may be able to operate the online business from home and a fixed premises may not be required at all. Alternatively, the entrepreneur may choose to locate in a much cheaper site in a more out of the way location, where strong road links and sufficient amounts of cheap labour are readily available.

 Exam Gold The factors influencing business location is an easily accessible topic for many students. It is very important that when considering factors of location, you review the circumstances of the individual business in the case study very carefully. Repeating factors that you have learnt from textbooks may not always be appropriate for the business in the question, so it is vital to apply your knowledge effectively to each business situation in order to maximise your marks.

1.4.3 THE MARKETING MIX

What you need to know

What the marketing mix is and the importance of each element (price, product, promotion, place)

How the elements of the marketing mix work together (balancing the marketing mix based on the competitive environment, the impact of changing consumer needs on the marketing mix, the impact of technology on the marketing mix: e-commerce, digital communication)

What the marketing mix is and the importance of each element

The marketing mix consists of four elements: Price, Product, Promotion and Place. Each of these factors are combined and used by a business to encourage customers to buy products from them. It is known as a "mix" because each part affects the others. The mix must be integrated and suitable to appeal to the target customer.

Price

Price refers to how much the customer will pay to buy the product. Customers want value for money and for the price to reflect the quality of the product. Price can be a very important part of the marketing mix when there are a lot of substitute products in the market. In this case, prices will need to remain low and in line with rivals.

However, the price becomes a less important factor of the marketing mix when a product is more desirable and unique than rival products. In this case, customers may be more willing to pay higher prices so a business can then charge more.

Product

The product refers to the good or service that the business produces. Before an entrepreneur decides on the specific product to sell, careful market research should be carried out to ensure that sufficient demand exists in the market to make the product viable.

Promotion

Promotion refers to the ways in which a business tries to persuade customers to buy a product. This could be through advertising, special offers, branding, sponsorship or product trials. Social media is increasingly used by small businesses to promote their products and businesses to a wide audience.

Place

Place relates to how a product is distributed to enable customers to access and buy it easily. This may be through the internet, physical stores or both. The nature of the business will impact the channel or method of distribution chosen by the entrepreneur.

 Exam Gold Students often confuse place in the marketing mix and link it to the factors affecting business location rather than the different channels of distribution that businesses use to access their customers and sell their products. It is important that you do not fall into this trap. Strong subject knowledge is absolutely vital for exam success, so you must revise carefully.

How the elements of the marketing mix work together

Balancing the marketing mix based on the competitive environment

An effective marketing mix will be balanced and integrated. This means that all of the elements should work together consistently so that a logical message is provided to the customer about each product.

Every marketing mix will be different and competition can have a significant impact on the marketing mix that is chosen by a business. This means that one or two elements of the mix may be more important than the others due to the competition in the market. For example, a new hairdressing business that opens in an area with already established hairdressers may focus on changing the service enough from rivals to make it different. This could be through offering an organic hairdressing service and high-quality products, rather than competing on other factors such as price. In contrast, a fast food business surrounded by many other fast food businesses may focus on price and ensuring a delivery service is available to attract customers.

The impact of changing consumer needs on the marketing mix

Consumer needs are constantly changing and as a result it is important that the marketing mix is also flexible. A product that has a rigid marketing mix which does not respond to changing needs will ultimately see a fall in sales volume, as the product will not be in demand. It is, therefore, important for businesses to continually monitor customer needs and adapt their marketing mix appropriately. For example, a café may decide to offer a takeaway service for customers as consumer lifestyles are increasingly busy and the need for greater convenience increases.

The impact of technology on the marketing mix

Technology is constantly changing and every business should actively monitor these changes in terms of how the marketing mix should be adapted.

E-commerce

E-commerce refers to online trading. M-commerce is online trading via a mobile device, such as a mobile phone.

The growth of e-commerce and m-commerce has led to many businesses choosing to operate online, as a physical retail outlet is not required. This has affected place in the marketing mix.

The online share of retail sales in the UK in 2019 was 19% and the forecast growth rate of online shopping in 2023 is 34.5%. The UK has the most advanced e-commerce market in Europe. Smartphones are the main devices that generate the largest share of revenue online. In terms of the marketing mix this means that businesses must ensure their websites are user friendly, easy to navigate, up-to-date and that payment systems are efficient and convenient, in order to win sales from rivals.

Digital communication

Digital communication is any form of communication that takes place electronically, for example through websites, email and social media.

Digital communication has a large impact on the marketing mix, particularly promotion. Customers can easily access websites and different forms of social media to find information about a business, its products and customer reviews. This may then impact whether customers decide to buy from that business or not. It is important that businesses actively manage digital communication successfully by employing appropriately skilled staff, as negative messages can be seen by many people and in the worst cases go viral. This can have a long-term impact on the reputation of the business, sales and revenue.

The popularity of online and price comparison sites means that customers are now able to compare prices and/or reviews about a good or service extremely quickly. This can help them make an informed choice about which product to purchase. This highlights again the importance of businesses ensuring that all information displayed on websites is up-to-date and relevant.

Exam Gold The marketing mix is covered in more depth in Theme 2. For this part of the specification, ensure you have a clear understanding of each of the different elements of the marketing mix and how they must integrate together to be effective. For example, it would not make sense to sell a product in a value store at a high price.

You must remember the marketing mix is not static, it will constantly change with technology, customer needs and the actions of competitors. A business that adapts to these external factors is much more likely to be successful in the long term.

1.4.4 BUSINESS PLANS

What you need to know

The role and importance of a business plan (to identify the business idea, business aims and objectives, target market (market research), forecast revenue, cost and profit, cash-flow forecast, sources of finance, location, marketing mix)

The purpose of planning business activity (the role and importance of a business plan in minimising risk and obtaining finance)

The role and the importance of a business plan

A business plan is a document that is produced by entrepreneurs to help coordinate the planning and start-up of a business. Through the production of a business plan the business is more likely to be successful, as it will highlight how the business will survive against competition in the market. Business plans can also be produced by existing businesses that are looking to expand or change.

The main parts of a business plan, in context of a business start-up, are explored below.

The business idea

A description of the proposed business idea including how it will be different from rivals.

Business aims and objectives

Aims and objectives show the general goals that the business will strive to achieve and will, therefore, give direction and a purpose to the business. The objectives should be SMART and show how the aims of the business will be met.

Target market (market research)

Reliable market research will help an entrepreneur to identify its key target customers in, hopefully, a growing market that the business has chosen to set up in. This will help to increase the chances of business success and ensure that any promotional activity is effective in meeting its aims.

Forecast revenue, cost and profit

An entrepreneur will need to skilfully breakdown forecast costs into fixed and variable to help predict with greater accuracy the costs the business is likely to incur. This is important as it will directly impact the level of profit that the business can make. Market research will need to be undertaken to predict demand and, therefore, likely sales volume for the business. This will then allow the entrepreneur to forecast revenue.

Knowing this information will enable the entrepreneur to estimate the level of break even output for the business. This is important information as it allows the entrepreneur to make key decisions regarding the sales price and its costs. A start-up business is likely to set financial aims/objectives linked to survival, break even, sales and profit.

Cash-flow forecast

In order for the new business to survive, it is important that a cash-flow forecast is included in the business plan so that a business is able to prepare for periods when there is likely to be a cash deficit. It would be wise for an entrepreneur to be cautious when predicting inflows and very realistic when forecasting cash outflows. This will help to ensure that the actual cash figures are in line, as much as possible, with forecast predictions.

Sources of finance

The amount of finance required for the business start-up will need to be included in the business plan, as well as the proposal as to where the entrepreneur is anticipating to gain the required funds. It is expected that the entrepreneur would invest a significant amount of personal savings to show commitment to the business idea.

Location

The proposed location of the business will depend upon many factors, such as the nature of business activity and the proximity to the market or rivals. It is a balance of these factors, alongside the cost, which will determine the location of the business. This is a key consideration in business planning.

Marketing mix

Each element of the marketing mix will need to be considered for the product offerings the new business is planning to sell. The entrepreneur will need to ensure that all elements of the mix will integrate together which will enable the business to compete effectively in its market.

Exam Gold This section covers many of the topics already covered in Theme 1. Double check your understanding of these key areas and, if you are unsure, go back and revisit those sections again.

The purpose of planning business activity

The role and importance of a business plan in minimising risk and obtaining finance

The production of a business plan will be of huge importance to a new business start-up for a number of reasons:

- It will reduce risk, as it will ensure that all elements of the business have been thought about before setting up. In theory, this should mean that the business will not experience any unexpected surprises.
- It can act as a checklist that the owner can follow to ensure that the business is on track with its plans. If not, the entrepreneur can then make decisions to correct any problems.
- It will help the entrepreneur to monitor progress to see whether the aims/objectives have been met in the time scale set.
- It will increase the sources of finance available to an entrepreneur. A well-produced business plan may result in the bank being more willing to offer a loan at a lower rate of interest or a venture capitalist being encouraged to invest in the business. If the business is looking for other investors, this will be a key document to help it in its quest.

Exam Gold Business planning is a popular topic area which is regularly examined. It is worth remembering that you will not be expected to know the format of a business plan nor will you be asked to produce one. Questions that will appear will focus on the role and importance of business planning for a small business and the identification of its different elements.

It is important to recognise that, just because a business plan is produced, it will not automatically guarantee business success. A business plan needs to be carefully thought through and followed. Equally, an entrepreneur that sticks rigidly to a plan without allowing flexibility to adapt to any external or internal changes in the business, will not benefit from its production. Without doubt, a business plan is useful to produce, but it must not stifle creativity and entrepreneurship when setting up a business.

UNDERSTANDING EXTERNAL INFLUENCES ON BUSINESS

1.5 UNDERSTANDING EXTERNAL INFLUENCES ON BUSINESS

Section 1.5 examines the key stakeholders of businesses and their different objectives. Technological change, different types of legislation and how developments in the wider economy impact business are also explored.

1.5.1 BUSINESS STAKEHOLDERS

What you need to know

Who business stakeholders are and their different objectives (shareholders (owners), employees, customers, managers, suppliers, local community, pressure groups, the government)

Stakeholders and businesses (how stakeholders are affected by business activity, how stakeholders impact business activity, possible conflicts between stakeholder groups)

Who business stakeholders are and their different objectives

A stakeholder is anyone who has an interest in, or is affected by, business activity. Each group of stakeholders will have different objectives, as they will want different things from the business. The key stakeholder groups in a business and their specific objectives are shown in the table.

Stakeholder group	Objectives of different stakeholder groups
Shareholder (owners)	• In smaller businesses, long term growth and success is usually a priority • In larger businesses with shareholders, a high level of profits and dividends are of high importance
Employees/ Managers	• Fair pay and good perks, or fringe benefits, such as staff discount • Job security and good working conditions through the long-term success of the business • Promotion opportunities • Job satisfaction and status through high levels of motivation, interesting roles and responsibilities
Customers	• Value for money • Product quality that meets customer expectations • Appropriate levels of customer service • Choice and innovative products
Suppliers	• Honest and fair trading, particularly related to prices and trade credit • Prompt payments • Continued placement of orders • A strong two-way relationship with good communication

Table continues on the next page

Local community	• Long-term success of the business to create and retain jobs • Compliance with local laws and regulations, for example noise, pollution etc.
Pressure groups	• Honest and fair trading from businesses, particularly related to the environment and customers
The government	• Prompt and correct payment of taxes • Creation of jobs through business growth • Compliance with business legislation

 Exam Gold Students often muddle the terms 'stakeholder' and 'shareholder.' A shareholder is a part owner of a company and is an example of a stakeholder. Remember: revise all key terms carefully to avoid these common errors.

Stakeholders and businesses

How stakeholders are affected by business activity

Any activity of a business will affect some, if not all of its stakeholders. The impact will differ dependent on the particular stakeholder group. The impact may be positive for some stakeholders and negative for others, or a mixture of both. For example, a negative impact on the local community of living near a popular pub could be higher levels of noise pollution, particularly in the evening. However, in contrast, the local community may benefit from charitable donations made by the business, such as sponsoring the local football team, which will help to bring a sense of community to the area.

How stakeholders impact business activity

Whether a stakeholder will be able to impact business activity will depend upon the power of the specific stakeholder group. If a stakeholder group has a large amount of power, it is more likely that it will be able to influence the actions of a business, for example, a key customer threatening to take their orders to another business than another group that has less power, and, therefore, is of less importance to a business, such as the local community for a web design business. Some stakeholder groups will have more interest in the activities of a business than others. This will depend upon the nature of the business.

It is important that a business considers the objectives of the stakeholder groups with a high level of interest and power when making decisions, to ensure that they are fulfilled as much as possible.

Possible conflicts between stakeholder groups

Conflict can arise between different stakeholder groups because their objectives differ. For example, an objective for a business start-up of achieving survival would be supported by nearly all the stakeholders. Other than its competitors, it is unlikely to be in any other stakeholder's interest for a business to fail.

 Exam Gold Be prepared for questions in the exam to ask for specific examples of how stakeholders are affected by business activity, how stakeholders impact business activity and the possible conflicts that can arise.

For example, a 3 mark 'explain' question may ask for an example of a conflict between stakeholders. A good and straightforward example to use in this type of question would be the conflict that can exist between the owners of the business and employees. "Employees typically want more pay. (1st mark) This will increase costs of the business, which may negatively impact the level of profits. (2nd mark) This may conflict with the owners who commonly want high profits." (3rd mark)

Different types of technology used by business (e-commerce, social media, digital communication, payment systems)

How technology influences business activity (sales, costs, marketing mix)

Different types of technology used by business

Technology is ever-changing and businesses that adapt to these changes better than rival businesses may benefit from a competitive advantage.

There are many different types of technology that are used in business.

E-commerce

E-commerce is the sale of goods online. M-commerce is online trading via a mobile device, such as a mobile phone. Online trading is growing at a very fast rate. This trend has accelerated in 2020 for goods such as food and clothing.

However, not all products are suitable to sell online. A small business that makes personalised wedding dresses will need to physically engage with customers face-to-face in order to successfully meet customer needs.

There are many benefits to businesses of operating online, if the nature of the business activity allows:

- Opportunity to sell products 24 hours a day, 7 days a week
- Costs can be reduced, as there is less need for retail premises and no requirement to locate in areas with high rent
- The market can be expanded on a national and international basis
- The quality of the goods and efficiency of the business may be improved due to increased competition
- Data recording and analysis is easily achieved which can help with targeted promotional activity

However, there are some drawbacks:

- No personal contact with customers
- ICT systems have to be established, maintained and updated which can add to costs and lead to customer frustration if they are unreliable
- Distribution costs can increase rapidly through the increased geographical spread of sales
- Increased competition
- Providing good customer service, including product returns, can be expensive

Social media

Social media, such as Facebook, Twitter and Instagram, can be used to allow two-way communication between the business and a variety of different stakeholders, including customers and potential customers. Social media can generate increased awareness of a business and its products. It is not expensive to set-up and use at a basic level. This makes it popular with smaller businesses, as it can lead to increased demand and sales.

However, it is important that enough attention is paid to managing social media accounts through suitably trained staff, as any negative information or messages can easily be shared. This can affect the reputation of the business.

Digital communication

Digital communication is any form of communication that takes place electronically, for example through email, text and social media. Digital communication can be used in many ways by different stakeholders, for example:

- Customers – placing orders, requesting product information
- Suppliers – placing orders, payment of goods
- Employees – business announcements, communicating hours to be worked, payment of wages
- Shareholders – reports on business performance, dividend information and payments

Whilst digital communication is cheap and fast, there is a danger that it can lead to communication overload and the message being lost.

Payment systems

The growth of e-commerce has led to the increasing use of debit and credit cards to pay for goods online. Firms, such as PayPal, have developed to make this process easier and safer. Apple Pay and Google Pay are examples of contactless payment methods. Contactless payment is a secure method for consumers to purchase products using a debit, credit or smartcard. Contactless payments do not require a signature or PIN and therefore the transaction sizes on the cards are limited. Currently, this is £45.00 in the UK. Many businesses use electronic payment systems to pay staff directly into their bank accounts.

For businesses, electronic payment systems are convenient and efficient in terms of receiving and paying out money. However, there are disadvantages. The risk of fraud has resulted in some customers being unwilling to input their payment details on line. There is also the cost of buying and maintaining the systems.

Exam Gold You will not be expected to know lots of details about various forms of social media or payment systems. Just make sure you are able to name different types of social media and payment systems and you are clear how they are used in business.

How technology influences business activity

Sales

The convenience to customers of using technology to buy goods and services gives businesses the opportunity to increase their sales. The popularity of e-commerce has allowed small firms to access wider markets than would otherwise be possible if they operated solely from fixed premises. This clearly increases sales and is a trend that is set to continue into the future.

Technology can also be the foundation of the products and/or the business itself. Web design, app development and online travel consultants are all examples of businesses that have developed due to changes in technology.

Costs

Businesses will experience increased costs of adopting and maintaining technology. However, dependent on the type of business, it may be a cost that cannot be ignored. Failing to implement technology can place a business at a disadvantage to rivals if, for example, competing firms adopt more convenient payment systems. This may encourage customers to trade with them rather than a business that does not invest in such technology.

However, a business can experience a reduction in costs through the use of technology, as it can make the business more efficient. For example, collecting online payments rather than dealing with cash that would need to be taken to the bank each day.

Marketing mix

Technology will affect the marketing mix of every business differently. As technology enables customers to check the prices of competing products easily online, it is important that a business pays enough attention to pricing decisions to help generate sales.

Technology can affect the processes of the business which, in turn, can increase efficiency. This can include the way products are made. Technology also opens up opportunities for businesses to generate sales through the development of new products or the adaptation of existing products. Mobile phones are a good example of this.

Technology allows data to be collected about customers through the use of customer loyalty cards and via online purchases. With this information, promotional activity can be more efficiently and effectively targeted at the correct target market.

Technology has resulted in a shift in the importance of online distribution. As sales increasingly move online, businesses have developed to take advantage of this trend and the opportunities that it presents. Firms such as Deliveroo and Just Eat allow small takeaway businesses to receive orders online which they would otherwise not be able to gain. Deliveroo or Just East then deliver these orders to the customers' doorsteps.

Exam Gold Technology is ever-changing. Businesses will need to choose which technology to invest in to ensure that a competitive advantage can be gained against rival businesses. A business that can operate more efficiently through the use of technology will have a lower cost base, after the cost of technology has been covered. These lower costs will enable a business to charge lower prices, giving the firm an advantage over competitors. Alternatively, in this situation a business can keep prices the same and make a bigger profit on each item sold. However, cost is clearly a big consideration which smaller businesses need to be very wary of when thinking about introducing new technology.

1.5.3 LEGISLATION AND BUSINESS

What you need to know

The purpose of legislation (principles of consumer law: quality and consumer rights, principles of employment law: recruitment, pay, discrimination and health and safety)

The impact of legislation on businesses (cost, consequences of meeting and not meeting these obligations)

The purpose of legislation

Governments introduce legislation in many areas of the economy. This is done to control businesses that otherwise might put profits before looking after its customers or treating its employees fairly. It also ensures a fair system, as all businesses in the UK have to meet the same legal requirements and therefore a 'level playing field' is created.

Principles of consumer law

Consumer law exists to try and protect consumers and their interests.

Quality

Consumer law requires that all products a business sells must be 'fit for purpose,' of reasonable quality and safe. The product must therefore work as it should and be free from defects.

Consumer rights

As well as being 'fit for purpose' and of reasonable quality, products must be described accurately and reflect the product being sold. This requirement is included in the Trade Descriptions Act, 1968.

The Consumer Rights Act 2015, states that if businesses, large or small, do not meet their legal requirements, consumers are entitled to a refund, as long as proof of purchase can be shown. It is the responsibility of the business that sold the goods to resolve any issues, not the manufacturer. If a service has been purchased, the service must be completed at a reasonable price and by the time stated. The customer can request that any unsatisfactory work is repaired or carried out again at no extra cost.

 Exam Gold There are many Acts of Parliament that aim to protect consumers when buying goods and services. Other laws include the Weights and Measures Act, which ensures that customers are buying the correct measurements of a product that is stated, and the Food Safety Act. This Act requires that staff in relevant industries have food hygiene training and business premises are inspected regularly for the correct hygiene standards.

Principles of employment law

Employment law aims to prevent businesses from discriminating against employees at work based on 'protected characteristics' such as sex, age, religion and disability.

It protects workers in four main areas: recruitment, pay, discrimination and health and safety.

Recruitment

The Equality Act 2010 makes it unlawful for employers to discriminate against job applicants (and existing workers) because of a protected characteristic. This means that a business can choose a candidate with a protected characteristic over one who does not if they are both suitable for the job. This only applies if the characteristic is underrepresented in the workplace, profession of industry or the person is at a disadvantage due to that characteristic. For example, if people from a certain ethnic group are not often given jobs in the sector that the business operates in.

However, a business cannot choose a candidate who is not as suitable for the job just because they have a protected characteristic.

Employment law also means that a business cannot:

- State or imply that it will discriminate against anyone in a job advert, for example advertising for a 'young person'
- Ask if a person is married, looking to have children or ask questions about any other protected characteristics
- Request information on date of birth, unless it is a requirement to carry out a particular job role, for example, to sell alcohol
- Ask about health or disability, unless there are necessary requirements of the job that cannot be met without reasonable adjustments to the workplace being made
- Refuse to employ someone based on a criminal conviction that has been served; the candidate does not need to tell the potential employer about any previous convictions

Pay

The Equal Pay Act 1970 states that employers must pay men and women the same for work of equal value and status. Sex discrimination is prohibited between employees in terms of their pay and the terms and conditions of employment, such as holiday pay. Despite the existence of this Act, there are still examples of women being paid less than men for work of the same value.

In 1999, legislation was brought in to guarantee that employees over 18 must be paid at least the National Minimum Wage (NMW) by law. This was extended in 2003 to include 16 and 17-year olds. Since April 2016, if staff members are aged 25 or over, they must be paid at least the National Living Wage (NLW). The NMW and NLW are reviewed and usually changed every year. The NLW was extended to include 23 and 24-year olds from April 2021 and will be extended again in 2024 to include 21 and 22-year olds.

Discrimination

As well as in recruitment, it is unlawful for businesses to discriminate against any employee based on the 'protected characteristics' in terms of selection for training and development, promotion and/or redundancy.

Health and safety

The Health and Safety at Work Act (1974) states that employers have the duty to ensure, as far as it is possible, the health, safety and welfare at work of all their employees and anyone visiting the business premises.

The Act requires:

- Safe operation and maintenance of the working environment, both machines and the building
- Safe use, handling and storage of dangerous substances
- Adequate training of staff to ensure health and safety
- Adequate welfare provisions for staff at work

Employees also have a legal duty to ensure that they co-operate with the business over health and safety matters and that they take reasonable care of themselves and others whilst at work.

The impact of legislation on businesses

Cost

The existence of legislation results in large amounts of paperwork for businesses to check that they are meeting the legal requirements successfully. This costs time and money which could be used elsewhere in the business. Increased costs lowers profits and can result in a business being forced to charge higher prices for products. This can make a small business uncompetitive, especially when larger firms may be able to make cost savings elsewhere, for example, through the bulk purchase of goods from suppliers.

Benefits of meeting these obligations

There are many benefits of meeting the requirements of consumer law:

- Improved reputation in the marketplace, leading to an increase in sales
- Bad publicity is avoided
- Less costs of repair, replacement and paperwork
- Fines can be avoided

Benefits of meeting the requirements of employment law:

- A more diverse workforce will be employed leading to better decision-making
- A wider pool of applicants may apply for job vacancies which may improve the calibre of the workforce
- Higher staff retention, as people want to remain working for the employer
- Increased productivity of employees, as staff are motivated to work in a safe environment

Businesses that do not meet the requirements of the law can be fined and gain bad publicity, which can damage the long-term reputation of the firm and reduce sales.

Exam Gold You are not required to have an in-depth understanding of legislation and particular laws. Therefore, focus your revision on the purpose of legislation and the impact it will have on business. Remember, all businesses in the UK have to follow the same laws, so no business can gain a cost advantage over another by not implementing the requirements stated in the legislation. However, if a business is competing internationally and each country has different requirements of the law, the increased costs of complying to legislation can make UK products uncompetitive if higher prices need to be charged to cover these costs.

1.5.4 THE ECONOMY AND BUSINESS

What you need to know

The impact of the economic climate on businesses (unemployment, changing levels of consumer income, inflation, changes in interest rates, government taxation, changes in exchange rates)

The impact of the economic climate on business

The economic climate broadly refers to how the UK economy is performing. It is measured by gross domestic product (GDP). GDP is the total value of goods and services produced by a country in a year. If the economy is doing well, more goods and services will be produced and sold and there will be more money spent and received by the government.

Economic growth will impact different areas of the economy.

Unemployment

The government will aim to have high employment and, therefore, low unemployment in the economy, so there will be less people reliant on benefit payments. When the economy is growing, there are more jobs available. At this time, workers may be more motivated to work harder, as they feel their jobs are secure.

When unemployment is low, employees may also see a wage increase. This is because there will be fewer staff available to fill job vacancies. To attract workers businesses may, therefore, need to increase pay levels. Staff may be more tempted to move jobs if they can gain more attractive pay and conditions of employment elsewhere. This may increase the costs of recruitment, training and development and wages for the business.

Changing levels of consumer income

If consumer incomes change, this will affect how much and which products they buy. If more people are in work, average income levels will be higher. As a result, consumers are likely to buy more non-essential products that they may view as luxuries. However, if unemployment rises and consumer incomes fall, some sectors of the economy will be harder hit. For example, the demand for eating out or going to the cinema may fall.

Inflation

Inflation is the general increase in prices and the fall in the purchasing power of money. Controlling inflation is one of the UK government's main economic targets.

Businesses are impacted by inflation through increased costs. The prices of goods and services will increase and, therefore, it is likely that employees will demand higher wages so that their standard of living can be maintained and they can afford to pay these higher prices.

However, to pay for increased costs, businesses may need to increase their selling prices. This may lower demand.

Changes in interest rates

Interest rates are the cost of borrowing charged by a lender or the reward for saving. Interest rates are measured as a percentage.

When interest rates increase, it means that the cost of borrowing increases. This will have the following effects:
- Business loans will be more expensive. This will discourage investment and may mean businesses become less competitive or are reluctant to expand or even set-up
- Costs may increase, as the cost of existing loans/overdrafts may be higher. This can lower demand as consumers spend less on non-essential products, as they may be required to make higher mortgage repayments
- Businesses and consumers may choose to save money to earn the higher interest, rather than spend it
- Consumers will spend less, as it is more expensive for them to borrow money to finance larger purchases, such as cars
- The exchange rate may increase, making the cost of goods sold by businesses to other countries (exports) more expensive in foreign markets

Government taxation

The government raises tax in many different ways. These include:
- Income tax, a tax charged on wages/salaries
- Corporation tax, a tax on the profits of incorporated businesses; sole traders and partnerships pay income tax on their profits
- VAT, a purchase tax charged on products that are bought; some items are zero-rated for VAT purposes, such as children's clothes

The government decides on the different tax levels and this is communicated in the budget. In general, if taxation increases, demand will fall for goods and services. The government uses taxation to pay for services that are controlled by the government, such as the NHS and state education. Increased spending in these areas may create more jobs and have a positive effect on the economy.

Changes in exchange rates

An exchange rate shows the value of one currency in relation to another. When a business trades internationally, it will need to pay for the products in the currency of the country that it buys the goods/services from. Changes in exchange rates will affect how much of the foreign currency can be bought per pound.

Imports are goods and services that are purchased from other countries. These might be raw materials or finished products or services purchased by consumers. Exports are goods and services sold to businesses and consumers in other countries.

If the exchange rate changes so that the currency appreciates, then it will be worth more. This means that it will cost more for businesses located outside of the UK to buy the UK currency, Pound Sterling. It will also be cheaper for businesses located in the UK to buy another country's currency. This means that imports into the UK will be cheaper and exports will become more expensive.

If a currency depreciates then it will be worth less and be cheaper for other countries and foreign businesses to buy. Fluctuations in exchange rates cause uncertainty in business and will, therefore, impact business decision-making. Long-term changes may discourage businesses from trading internationally, as it will impact on their profits.

Worked Example

A simple example is given to show the impact a change in exchange rates can have on a UK business trading with an American business:

Last month, the exchange rate was £1.00 (GBP) which could be exchanged for $1.60 American Dollars (USD). Now, the exchange rate has appreciated to £1.00 to $2.00 USD

A UK business imports raw materials from America each month worth $100 (USD). The appreciation in the exchange rate has resulted in a reduction of business costs for the UK business.

Last month, the UK business would need to have converted £62.50 of GBP to pay the American firm.

This is calculated by $100.00/$1.60 = £62.50.

However, this month, the same raw materials will cost the UK business £50.00.

This can be calculated by $100.00/$2.00 = £50.00.

This is positive for the UK business, as the reduction in costs may lead to an increase in profits. The business may also have more flexibility in its pricing, if the appreciation looks like it will continue into the future. If prices can be lowered, the business may be able to compete more effectively in its market.

Exam Gold

A very useful acronym to help you remember the impact an appreciation of exchange rates has on business is:

Strong
Pound
Imports
Cheaper
Exports
Dearer

You can reverse this acronym to show the impact if the pound depreciates against another currency:

Weak
Pound
Imports
Dearer
Exports
Cheaper

Exam Gold You do not need to know the reasons and the causes of any economic change. Your focus for revision should be on how changes in each of these economic factors will impact different sized businesses, particularly small firms. For example, how would a low-priced food retailer be affected by a fall in income tax? Demand may fall, as people can now afford more upmarket brands, which may lower the food retailer's revenue.

This is an area of the specification which is commonly examined. Remember, in 3-mark questions and above, you must include connectives in your response in order to show that you are demonstrating analytical skills through writing logical chains of reasoning. These topic areas are a great way to practise the skill of analysis.

1.5.5 EXTERNAL INFLUENCES

The importance of external influences on business (possible responses by the business to changes in technology, legislation and the economic climate)

The importance of external influences on business

External influences are those factors that are outside the control of a business but can impact them. Businesses must prepare as much as possible for any changes in external factors, which may be on a local, national or international scale. The businesses that are the most successful will have a clear plan in place as to how they will respond to any such changes.

Possible responses by the business to changes in:

Technology

Any advancements in technology need to be weighed up and measured carefully by the business to decide whether it wishes to invest in that piece of technology. Technology is always changing and it may not be possible for a business to invest in every type of technology that is developed. Cost, the finance available, competitor actions and the nature of the business itself will all be key considerations in whether a new piece of technology is adopted.

However, the huge increase in the use social media and e-commerce in society would make it very difficult for even the smallest business to ignore and not consider. Successfully thinking about what customers expect, and meeting these needs, will be at the forefront of any decision regarding technology.

Legislation

Businesses must ensure that they operate within the parameters of the law. Failure to do this could result in fines, bad publicity and a poor reputation which may be difficult to overcome in the future. Clearly legislation increases business costs, as time and money must be spent ensuring that businesses are compliant with the law.

However, it can be argued that legislation exists to protect consumers and workers, as well as to restrict the activities of unethical businesses. This may be considered a real positive in the UK. Businesses may be best to view any changes in legislation as favourable and ensure that they plan ahead and respond appropriately.

The economic climate

Every business and sector of the economy will be affected differently by changes in the economic climate. A business that trades internationally will be affected by fluctuations in exchange rates, but not every business is an importer or an exporter.

Every business, however, will be affected by changing levels of unemployment, consumer incomes, inflation, interest rates and government taxation. The degree to which a business is affected will depend upon the extent of the change in the economic conditions, for example how large any increase or decrease in taxation or interest rates happens to be.

It will also depend upon the nature of the business. For example, a business that sells luxury goods and a business that sells essential goods will be affected differently and, therefore, respond differently to a change in economic conditions. Businesses that sell luxuries will be much more affected by a change in the economic climate. For example, if there is a downturn in the economy, these businesses will see less demand, fewer sales, lower profits and, as a result, may need to make some staff redundant in order to survive. This will cause higher unemployment, which will further impact sales of businesses selling luxury products.

For these reasons, the careful management and stability of the economy is a key factor that governments prioritise. Businesses are more likely to invest and take risks when they are more certain of the future. Investment creates wealth and jobs and is, therefore, a situation that governments encourage.